KU-765-844

Illustrated by
Charlotte Trounce

DRESS

[WITH]

SENSE

with over 200 illustrations

Christina Dean
Hannah Lane
Sofia Tärneberg
(Redress)

Thames & Hudson

A percentage of the profits from the sale of this book go to
Redress, an environmental non-governmental organization
(NGO) working to reduce waste in the fashion industry

For those who went before us, who walk with us now and
those yet to come. If fashion is a reflection of our times,
may our legacy show that we loved style and sustainability
in equal measure.

First published in the United Kingdom in 2017
by Thames & Hudson Ltd, 181A High Holborn,
London WC1V 7QX

Dress [with] Sense © 2017 Thames & Hudson Ltd, London
Text © 2017 Redress Limited
Illustrations © 2017 Charlotte Trounce

Designed by Amélie Bonhomme and Amy Preston

All Rights Reserved. No part of this publication may
be reproduced or transmitted in any form or by any means,
electronic or mechanical, including photocopy, recording
or any other information storage and retrieval system,
without prior permission in writing from the publisher.

British Library Cataloguing-in-Publication Data
A catalogue record for this book is available from the
British Library

ISBN 978-0-500-29277-8

Printed and bound in China by C&C Offset Printing Co Ltd

To find out about all our publications, please visit
www.thamesandhudson.com. There you can subscribe
to our e-newsletter, browse or download our current catalogue,
and buy any titles that are in print.

Contents

In search of a conscious closet

It has been said that fashion is a reflection of our times. If this is true, then now is the time to 'redress' those reflections cast by our clothes and closets. The personal choices we make while shopping have a significant impact on society and the environment, and the way we buy, wear, care for and dispose of our clothes gives an active voice to our conscious selves.

Much of fashion today is all about ease of consumption, acquiring clothes as cheaply as possible, and having more, more and more of them. It is also one of the most environmentally polluting industries (second only to oil), as the production of clothes and textiles exploits natural resources and releases toxic chemicals into our waterways.[1]

The clothes we wear, from production to the consumer-use stage, when we wash, dry and (often) prematurely get rid of them, are emitters of carbon dioxide, fuelling the ongoing climate-change crisis. Added to this minefield of challenges are the issues of safe working conditions and fair wages. If we could trace the invisible threads that link our clothes back to the fields and farmers who produced the raw materials, and the factory workers who turned them into garments, we might discover a shocking trail of environmental and social devastation.

But it's not just how our clothes are produced that should set alarm bells ringing, it's also our failure to care for them properly. Skills such as mending, cleaning and storing are being lost, and our quest for cleanliness as we wash, dry and iron the clothes in our wardrobes represents 75–80 per cent of the total energy consumed in a garment's life cycle, from the time the plant fibres are grown to when the item is ultimately discarded.[2]

This leaves us at a fashion crossroads: we must decide how and where to change, and to reassess our relationship with our clothes. We are now more aware about the negative impacts of fashion, and it is possible to see the once-invisible threads that connect our clothes to pollution, waste and unfair working conditions. Turning a blind eye is no longer palatable. It is time to question whether we can continue to fill our closets with resource-guzzling, poorly made clothes.

As fashion consumers, we have the power to effect change. It is now considered not only fashionable to put consciousness back into our lifestyles, from what we eat to what we wear, but also the right thing to do, as more and more of us search for ways to lead mindful lives. Our all-important spending power, together with an increased awareness and desire to make ethical choices, arms us with the tools we need to strive for a more conscious closet.

Doing so does not mean rushing out to buy a completely new, ethical and sustainable wardrobe. Instead, it's about making small changes in the way we buy, care for and discard our clothes. These changes might seem time-consuming or overwhelming at first, but with some knowledge and a few guiding principles, you can push your closet towards stylish sustainability. It is important, too, to keep in mind the positive benefits of the fashion industry, such as economic development and a democratic access to clothes in all colours, shapes and sizes.

This guide will help you navigate your personal journey through the complex fashion landscape, and identify the issues you feel strongly about – whether discovering a meaningful brand or learning a new skill. You will discover that creating a conscious closet is as achievable for stylists and supermodels as it is for the rest of us. You can continue loving fashion and updating your wardrobe to reflect your changing tastes, but you will do so with a more considered approach, ensuring that your love of fashion doesn't cost the earth or her people, and that you feel as good on the inside as you look on the outside.

Christina Dean, Hannah Lane and Sofia Tärneberg (Redress)

'The global turmoil in the financial markets and rising unemployment is mirrored by the turmoil seen in climate change, food insecurity and the water crisis, and compounded by the end of the era of cheap oil. But there's an opportunity for us to use this period of reflection to find a sustainable advantage.'
Dilys Williams, Centre for Sustainable Fashion,
University of the Arts, London

'Deep down, everyone wants to make a difference. More consumers are waking up to the core truth that they want to look good, feel good and do good. Sustainability is now relevant and no longer considered fringe or alternative.'
Marci Zaroff, eco-fashion pioneer

Buy

The reality

Each time you buy an item of clothing, do you pause to consider – in that brief moment between handing over your cash and stashing your new top or pair of shoes in the carrier bag (or virtual shopping basket) – what is behind your purchase and what you are really buying into? Probably not, and you are not alone. Too often in today's fast-paced consumer culture we buy new clothes with little or no awareness about how or where they were made, or by whom.

Our lack of knowledge is partly caused by the complexity of the global fashion supply chains. Your cotton T-shirt may have originated in Mali, been processed in Malaysia, stitched in Mumbai and finished in Milan, before being sold to you in shops from Lima to London. Our clothing's supply chains are as mysterious as they are extensive, making the true environmental and social impact of buying clothes complex and difficult to comprehend.

Not only are we buying more, we are also buying cheaper. And when you buy cheap, that's what you get. Many of today's mass-produced, low-cost clothes are so devoid of quality that they quickly fall apart at the seams or hemlines. This lack of quality adds frustration to our mindless cycle of consumption, which ultimately leaves us dressed in poorly designed and produced clothes, made by sometimes poorly paid or treated workers and finished with toxic chemicals. This ill-considered buying behaviour is tearing out the heart, soul and style from our wardrobes.

The life cycle of our clothes

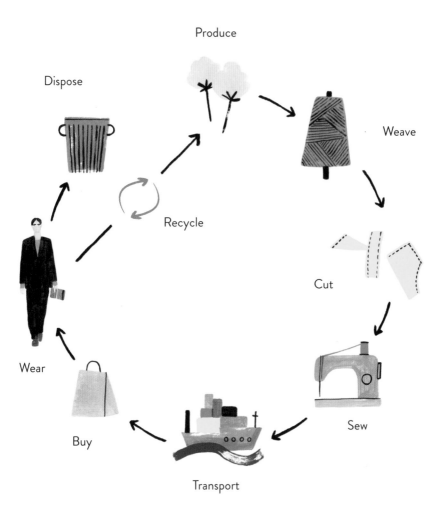

Produce

Dispose

Weave

Recycle

Cut

Wear

Sew

Buy

Transport

Here's what you need to know...

We buy too much

Over 150 billion new garments are made every year to meet our growing demand for clothing.[3] In the UK alone, sales of new clothing increased by 60 per cent in the first decade of this century, putting extreme pressure on the earth's natural resources.[4]

We buy more, but spend less

Despite the global market being valued recently at a whopping £2.3 trillion ($3 trillion), and the fact that our global spending on fashion and footwear is expected to increase by £46.4 billion ($60 billion) between 2010 and 2020, we are spending less of our individual annual income on clothes.[5] One hundred years ago, 17 per cent of our annual expenditure went towards clothes; today, it is less than 3 per cent.[6] Clothes have become cheaper, and therefore less of a significant financial outlay for the individual.

We buy on impulse

Around 40 per cent of clothes purchased by women are impulse buys, rather than considered investments to be worn for the long term.[7] This move towards quick-fix shopping is exacerbated by both low prices and the fast turnover of new trends.

We pay an unfair price

From an average T-shirt costing $14 (£11.37), the retailer's costs amount to only $5.67 (£4.60), with $3.69 (£3.00) spent on materials, $1.03 (£0.84) on freight and insurance, $0.65 (£0.53) on factory margins and overheads and $0.18 (£0.15) to the agent, leaving a meagre $0.12 (£0.10) for the garment workers' labour.[8] We should ask ourselves if it is acceptable for clothes to be so cheap.

We are disconnected

Nearly 67 per cent of the world's clothing exports and 57 per cent of textile exports are produced in developing countries, where labour and environmental laws can be lax, making it difficult to fully gauge the true cost of the clothes we buy.[9]

We pollute the environment

Growing the plant fibres and dyeing and finishing the resulting fabrics require a cocktail of chemicals that contaminate and pollute the environment. The growing of cotton, for example, counts for 10 per cent of the total pesticide use worldwide and 22.5 per cent of the total use of insecticides.[10] Additionally, an estimated 17–20 per cent of industrial water pollution comes from dyeing and treating textiles.[11]

The breakdown of a T-shirt

Materials

Freight and insurance

Factory margin

Agent

Workers' wages

Factory overheads

We drain natural resources

The production of clothing requires huge amounts of the earth's precious natural resources. The production of one pair of jeans alone requires around 3,625 litres (797 gallons) of water, 3 kg (7 lbs) of chemicals, 400 mJ (111 kilowatt hours) of energy and 13 m² (140 sq ft) of harvested land.[12]

Things you can do

Buying clothes with no consideration for the environmental impact simply must become a thing of the past. Practising better, more informed consumer behaviour will ensure that we use our power to exert a positive influence on the world, protecting the planet and respecting her people. How you choose to spend your money on clothes – from what you buy to where you buy them from – is a fundamental step towards turning your purchases into something more meaningful.

At first, the notion of buying more consciously may feel daunting, with issues from human welfare to air pollution adding to the long list of things to worry about. But even small changes can lead to big shifts. We have the power to be champions of change – we just need to exercise it! It's time to buy clothes in a more conscious manner, which will both lighten our load on the planet and our wallets. Sharing the message, too, will help increase awareness. So draw inspiration from the following shopping tips, which will leave you wearing your values proudly and stylishly on your sleeve.

The production of one pair of jeans

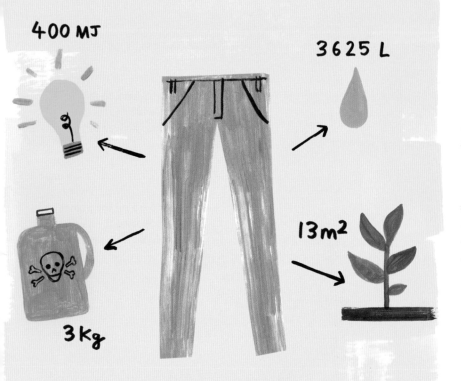

400 MJ

3625 L

3 kg

13 m²

Think before you shop

For many of us, shopping for clothes is a chaotic and impulsive experience. We get caught up in the thrill of the chase, or make the mistake of shopping when in a hurry or in a huff. Too often, we splash out on yet another bad buy that barely fits instead of something we genuinely like or can afford. By wising up to what we really want and what clothes work for our bodies, we can develop a wardrobe that suits us, while saving time, money and the planet.

2

Know your best features

Take note of the shapes and colours that most flatter your body and skin tone, and those outfits that draw the most compliments from admirers. By doing so, you'll feel more confident when buying similar items again. The better you look and feel in certain clothes, the more you will wear them.

1

Be aware of bad shopping habits

Have a good look at your favourite clothes and those you wear the most. The rest of your largely redundant wardrobe will reveal some bad habits. Identify what you haven't worn for a while and ask yourself if you bought it on impulse because it was in a sale or because it was a must-have trend, and if you bought it without trying it on. The next time you hit the shops, you will have a clearer idea of what will complement your existing wardrobe. As a result, you won't be burdened by unnecessary purchases that will be quickly relegated to the back of the closet.

'While working as a model, I learned that style has nothing to do with size. Knowing your body is essential, because you'll make better choices and focus on fit instead of size, and quality over quantity.'
Kate Dillon, model

3

Measure up

It is important to know your measurements. It may seem obvious, but many women don't know their waist size from their elbow. As sizes can vary between brands, knowing your measurements will reduce the time you spend trying on clothes in-store and make it easier when buying clothes online, and help you choose outfits that best fit your body. When clothes fit well, you'll wear them more and your wardrobe will have less waste. Hotspots to measure are your bust, chest, hips and waist.

4

Shop with intent

You are less likely to fall into the trap of impulse-buying if you shop with a clear goal in mind. Before heading out to the shops, make a list of gaps in your wardrobe to help you focus on the items you actually need and will complement what you already own. Identifying these items will reduce the amount of time you spend aimlessly browsing for clothes and leave you with more for wearing them.

DENISE HO

Having styled fashion shoots from New York to Hong Kong, Denise Ho now focuses on styling with a sustainable twist. Her clients include *Vanity Fair*, *Tatler* and *In Style* magazines and leading Chinese celebrities such as model Bonnie Chen (see pp. 204–6) and pop singer Kary Ng. Denise also advises companies around the world on how to integrate ethics into dressing for success.

'We often buy clothes with our eyes wide shut. I find that people get spurred on by impulse-buying trend-driven clothes that don't fit their bodies, let alone their lifestyles. Instead, it's essential to know the clothes that complement you best in order to maintain a stylish and sustainable wardrobe.'

Denise's essentials for successful shopping

Don't be a fashion victim

The trendy clothes that fill shop rails tend to be unique in style, colour and shape, which may not suit or fit everyone. This means that if you do buy the clothes, you won't get a lot of wear out of them, since trends move on so quickly.

Discover your personal style

Try on as many options as possible to see what works for you and what makes you feel comfortable.

Be inspired by other people

Even though I'm surrounded by clothes and fashion every day, I am still fascinated by how and why people put outfits together. The stories behind people's clothing choices are always inspiring, so don't be afraid to ask others for advice or tips.

China's celebrity stylist, Denise Ho, is both passionate and pragmatic when it comes to shopping without becoming a fashion victim. (See her tips on p. 23).

Wan & Wong Fashion, co-founded by EcoChic Design Award winner
Kelvin Wan, prioritizes sustainability by reusing factory textile waste.

Break bad shopping habits

Bad shopping habits, like succumbing to the thrill of an impulse buy or the buzz you get from owning the latest trend, are fuelled by the frenzy of marketing messages that constantly bombard us. Cracking them isn't easy. It requires willpower and recognizing the issues that drive your shopping, so that you can break the pattern.

Regardless of what you buy – including the most fair-trade, organic clothes out there – if you don't address your bad shopping habits then the cycle of over-consumption and overflowing wardrobes will continue, leading to enormous clothing waste. By breaking these habits and shopping with conviction, you will have a better closet to show for it.

'I vowed to avoid buying any "new" clothes for one year, and wear only vintage, recycled and repurposed couture instead. My revelation: clothes from previous decades were built to last, unlike today's fast-fashion designs.'
Bianca Alexander, creative director and host, Conscious Living TV

Borrow instead of buy

Sometimes we enthusiastically hit the shops searching for an expensive, one-off piece for a special occasion, which is then relegated to the back of the wardrobe once the night is over. Before reaching for your credit card, however, consider borrowing or renting, from friends or family, or from one of the impressive range of clothing-rental options out there, including Lena, Yeechoo and Filippa K's Lease the Look concept.

More and more clothing libraries have set up shop, both on the high street and online – and they are certainly not confined to bridal wear. These companies give you access to boutique-like collections, with timeless looks and current designs for both everyday and special occasions. By borrowing or renting, you get the look you're after for a fraction of the price, without the environmental footprint that comes with the production of yet another barely worn garment. And the same goes for you, too: open your wardrobe to friends and family to help make sharing the norm.

Buy less, buy better

It's as simple as that. The most sustainable shopping habit you can adopt is to buy fewer clothes that you will wear for longer. This means that the items you do buy are the best quality you can find, and are ones you really love and will wear for years to come. Remember, wearing the clothes you buy goes hand in hand with buying better. If you make a better choice and buy an organic T-shirt but hardly wear it, you are not building a conscious closet.

4

Scrutinize fabrics ...

When deciding whether or not to purchase an item of clothing, take a look at the material it is made from. Go for fabrics that look and feel durable: they will last longer owing to their higher colour-fastness and yarn strength, and will allow you to keep your clothes in the fashion loop and out of landfill (see chapter 4 for more on landfill). Look out for fabrics such as denim or Lyocell, and avoid delicate ones like chiffon, which can snag easily, and consider how they need to be cared for. Linings also help to reduce wear. Ask yourself if the garment will hold up after a few washes, and think about how you will clean, maintain and repair it.

3

Choose quality over quantity

The quality of our clothes is one of the most important factors in determining our closet's sustainability credentials. Too often clothes are made to last a season at best and, because of their inferior quality, can fall apart after their first spin in the washing machine. Good-quality clothes, however, are made from longer-lasting fabrics, with better cuts and finishing, making them the antithesis of their inferiorly produced, fast-fashion cousins. Before handing over your cash, consider how long your proposed purchase will stay active in your wardrobe. Is it well made and durable? Will you still be wearing it in a few years? If the answer is no, then the garment is not for you.

... and seams

Just as beauty is only skin-deep, don't be fooled by a garment's outer appearance. Instead, turn it inside out and have a good look. Well-made clothes have strong seams, hems, stitching and finishing; sloppily made garments will have loose stitching that can quickly unravel. When it comes to stitches, size matters! Smaller stitches grasp the fabric more sturdily than longer ones. Overlocking stitches, with a double run of stitching along the seam line and dense loops that 'hug' the seam, add extra strength. When in doubt, tug the seams gently before you buy. If the fabric begins to separate easily, you know you're looking at a poor job. Finally, clothes with larger seam widths (seam allowances) are easier to take in or let out, ensuring your clothes can grow or shrink along with your body.

Versatility is key

Consider how the item you want to buy will fit in with the other clothes you own, and how you will style it. Does it go with anything else in your wardrobe? Do you already have something similar? Buying versatile clothing that can be worn and styled in a variety of different ways will maximize your investment and minimize unnecessary waste (see chapter 3 for inspiration on how to style your clothes).

Get a reality check

When shopping for clothes, we tend not to think about the long-term life of the items we buy. The reality is that we wear clothes that fit comfortably into our lifestyles more often than we wear those that don't – and consequently wear only a fraction of the clothes in our wardrobes. Think about comfort and ease: if the garment in question tugs, scratches or restricts movement or breathing, you are unlikely to wear it much. So don't buy it. If you're tempted to buy clothes that don't suit how you really live, you will be wasting both money and resources.

Try it on

Always try clothes on when you shop. Like moods and the weather, sizes are changeable, according to designer or brand, and even fabric. It also pays to check the fit in-store, because while tailors can address many problems to do with ill-fitting clothes, their services come at a cost. When shopping for a jacket or coat, for example, pay attention to the fit around the shoulders, since adjusting this is a difficult, and therefore costly, alteration to make.

Resistance is better than regret

It is important to recognize that retailers want you to shop. When you see 'Sale' signs or 'Last Chance to Buy' splashed throughout the store and your email in-box is full of cheap deals, take a deep breath and resist. Before you reach the till with your prospective purchase, ask yourself if you really need it, or if you already own something similar. Can you afford it? Will it be out of fashion next month? Resisting quick-purchase thrills will be rewarded by the longer-term satisfaction of having a more stylish and wearable wardrobe.

10

Avoid retail 'therapy'

Shopping to cure feelings of boredom, frustration or sadness leads – more often than not – to impulsive, emotionally driven shopping decisions, leaving you with bags full of clothes you don't want or need, and provide only a temporary cure for feelings that are still there. Just as you would avoid shopping for food while hungry, so too should you avoid clothes shopping to make you feel better, which just results in overconsumption. Bad moods are bad for the planet! It's better to avoid the shops and look instead at other ways of lifting your mood – whether through friends, family or favourite activities (just not shopping!)

11

Walk away

When in doubt, don't. If you are wavering on the edge of buying or not buying, and you're simply not sure if you really like or need something enough to hand over your cash, exert your own authority and walk away. Take a coffee break, browse in other shops or, even better, sleep on it – particularly good advice for those of us who are susceptible to a bit of late-night online shopping. With the benefit of distance and time, you'll be a better judge of your needs, which will lead to more careful consumption and a more conscious closet.

Choose consciously

Despite living, breathing and sleeping in them, we know very little about where our clothes actually come from. As a result, few of us have a clue about how much they should cost. The reality is that we don't pay enough to compensate for the real (much higher) social and environmental costs caused by the production of our clothes.

With the new awakening in consumers' collective consciousness, however, we can make amends. There are stylish, more sustainable clothing options out there, from secondhand or recycled to organic. Whether stocking up on basics or making a once-in-a-lifetime purchase, you can choose clothes that ensure your closet has a lower environmental and more positive social impact. Unfortunately, there isn't one perfect sustainable clothing solution – all consumption has an impact – but there are any number of conscious shopping choices you can make, and they all start with the desire to wear your inner sensibilities on your sleeve.

1

Get informed

Knowledge is power. Seek information about your purchases, brands you already love and new brands you have your eye on. Ask where and how the clothes were made, and what they are made from. Find out if the brand has any environmental or social policies in place. Shop assistants may not have all of the answers, or indeed any, and the brands may not share much information on their labels, so you may need to extend your search to the brands' websites – you might be pleasantly surprised by the amount of information available. Alternatively, get someone else to do the probing for you and follow the growing number of stylish and informative sustainable fashion blogs online.

Consider the real cost

Clothes have become so cheap that we consume recklessly, without pausing to consider the consequences for the planet and the people who make them. The production of cheap clothing by necessity can mean cutting corners in the supply chain. Sadly, the first areas to feel the squeeze are often safe working conditions and adequate environmental protection. There are some key questions to ask yourself when considering such a purchase. How can the item be so cheap? Was it likely to have been made under fair working conditions? Is it possible to determine the environmental impact of its production? It may be difficult to get to the bottom of all these questions, but this shouldn't stop us from asking them.

3

Go beyond the brand

Over 60 per cent of clothes today are produced in countries so geographically and culturally far from home that they might as well be from Mars as Malaysia.[13] But going beyond the brand will remove the blinkers when buying. Check out marketing communications for mentions of the supply chain. Some brands produce clothes in space-age factories, with sustainable wastewater treatment systems, solar-powered energy, air dyeing, digital printing and blue-chip recycling facilities, while others list full details about their suppliers, sometimes with stories about specific workers, so that you can put a face to your pair of jeans. Still others focus on local production, which reduces clothing miles, provides employment and benefits the local economy, and may even ensure fairer working conditions that are easier to monitor.

Buy secondhand

Buying pre-loved clothes is one of the most cost-effective and sustainable ways of creating a conscious closet. What's not to love? You're practically guaranteed that no one else will be dressed the same and you'll pay a fraction of what you would when the garment was new. Finally, your closet will have a low environmental impact, because you are reusing resources already embedded in pre-existing clothes, rather than driving the production of new ones. Access to secondhand clothing is relatively easy through vintage shops and online shopping platforms. The icing on the cake is that if you buy from charity shops, you're also supporting good causes. If you're new to the vintage scene, you'll need to set aside more time as shopping for secondhand clothes needs perseverance, patience and plenty of creativity.

6

Be aware of chemicals

Pesticides, dyes and finishing chemicals, including Chromium VI, formaldehyde and azo-dyes, are embedded into the fabric of our clothes. But these chemicals also find their way into the ecosystem where they are produced. Later, they are sloshed into waterways closer to home each time we run the washing machine. To avoid this, look for organic fabrics that don't use deadly pesticides during the farming stage. Organic clothes are relatively easy to find because they are stocked by many high-street and luxury brands. But just because the cotton is organic doesn't guarantee that other toxic dyes and finishing chemicals weren't used. There are a growing number of eco-dyes made from natural ingredients, but their availability is more limited. You could also check if a particular brand has signed up to any standards, such as Oeko-Tex, Global Organic Textile Standards or bluesign, to ensure that your clothes are safer both for you and for the environment.

5

Look for alternatives

The reality is that all of the fabrics used in fashion, from cotton to silk, have some sort of impact. But there are alternatives available that tread more lightly on the earth than their conventional counterparts. Among these are recycled fabrics, made from anything from recycled cotton to wool to plastic bottles. Buying clothes made from recycled fabric saves the natural resources already invested in the original fibres, so you are helping to ease pressure on the environment by reducing the demand for new ones. Other alternatives include Tencel, made with fibres from trees with a low environmental footprint, and sustainable rubber and organic cotton. You can even buy clothes made from the waste products of milk, tea, coffee and coconuts. By choosing alternative fabrics, you will be investing in a more conscious closet, while also encouraging brands to come up with new innovations.

Consider animal ethics

The use of animal-derived materials (leather, wool, angora, fur, reptile skins, and so on) are found in products from both the high street and luxury. But as animal-welfare regulations and standards vary across the world from humane to horrific, it can be difficult to know what sort of conditions the animals were kept in before being turned into your shoes, belts or jumpers. Some animals may have been plucked and skinned alive; others crammed in cages and pumped with chemicals. This makes the wearing of animal products akin to walking an ethical tightrope.

Leather, one of the most polluting materials used in fashion, is widely available today and can be bought relatively cheaply. Because of this, the market for leather in fashion has expanded, and more cattle farming

is moving to developing countries, where animal-welfare laws can be weaker. And just because a label says 'Made in Italy', it doesn't mean that the cow who supplied the skin for your clutch actually came from Italy, but that the final construction took place there. So exercise caution when buying animal products: ask questions, search beyond the label or consider alternatives, such as vegan 'leather' and fake fur, from companies such as Matt & Nat. Look out for responsibly sourced leather (O My Bag is a good place to start) or, even better, choose secondhand.

Shop with a mission

Shopping may sometimes seem like an indulgent treat, but it can also be an act of conscientious sharing. There are socially orientated fashion business models emerging, such as FEED and TOMS, which are based on a sharing system: if you purchase a pair of shoes, for example, another pair is donated to someone in need. The beauty of these businesses is that you get to address your own clothing needs and at the same time trigger a donation elsewhere. But make sure you still have a genuine need to shop, and that you don't get caught up in the mission alone.

Support sustainable skills

Put your money where your mouth is: look out for sustainable design and wear it! In recent years, there has been an explosion in innovation, now being manifested in the work of designers around the world. Some are using zero-waste, upcycling and reconstruction design techniques, while others are reviving traditional skills such as embroidery, weaving and beadwork, which declined in the 19th and 20th centuries because of mechanization (check out Rags2Riches and Angus Tsui). Buying products made using these skills not only supports their continued existence, but also the workers – often women, and often living in developing countries – who make them.

Look at the labels

Always check the label. Although the information provided may be limited, you should be able to see where the garment was made and from what fabrics. Knowing the fabric will at least give you an idea about how to care for it, which will then guide your decision about whether or not to buy it. Occasionally, brands will also share their product's sustainability credentials. But a dose of caution is necessary, as some branding vocabulary – 'natural' and 'eco', for example – are often used loosely. If in doubt, look for more information to back up the brand's claims and ask staff where you can find out more.

11

Look for signs of authenticity

Some brands use standards or certifications – logos or marks on the labels and hangtags, issued by neutral third-party organizations – to provide verification about sustainability, social or ethical claims. These standards, including Global Organic Textile Standard, Global Recycle Standard and Fairtrade, are intended to give consumers confidence, since a company must undergo rigorous testing in order to get them. More brands are taking ownership of their entire supply chains, and are now able to provide detailed information about a product's process from start to finish – enabling you, if you wish, to trace the wool of your jumper back to the very sheep who provided it.

12

Start with the basics

Underwear, socks, tights and tops are the items we tend to replace the most and, because of regular use and washing, they often have shorter lifespans. It's therefore a good idea to start phasing in more sustainable options by exchanging your ordinary cotton pants for organic ones, and your tights for those made from recycled polyester. Because we buy these basics more frequently, small changes have a bigger impact. The good news is that sustainable basics are becoming more widely available from high-street brands, including H&M and Marks & Spencer.

13

Love it or leave it

Unfortunately, there isn't one perfect, completely sustainable product on the market. So in your pursuit of a conscious closet, don't be tempted to buy something you're not really keen on just because it is organic, recycled or Fairtrade. Usability must always come first, and it's better to buy something that you really love and will wear, regardless of what it is made from. Another way of looking at it is this: let's say you buy an organic, locally made garment produced in a solar-powered factory, with 20 per cent of the profits going to charity. Sound ideal? But if you never wear it, you are still wasting resources.

AMBER VALLETTA

Over the last 25 years, Amber Valletta has graced the covers of countless magazines and worked with the top designers in the business. More recently, she has made the move from modelling to acting, with film roles in *Hitch*, *What Lies Beneath* and *The Spy Next Door*. Amber produced and starred in the documentary series *Driving Fashion Forward*, and in 2013 launched the lifestyle brand Master & Muse by Amber Valletta. She currently serves as mentor for the CFDA + Lexus Fashion Initiative.

'We're not buying timeless or heirloom pieces, we're buying lots of stuff – with no thought. We think that a cheap T-shirt is the answer because we got a good deal, but ultimately, there's a price we're going to pay somewhere along the way. The reality is we don't have the luxury to be thoughtless consumers any longer.'

Amber's essentials for buying better

It's fashion-forward to buy better

I am committed to buying better by making better choices when I shop for clothes. What does it mean to buy better? It means I choose to buy products from brands that tell you how and where their clothes are made, and that contribute positively to the world. Being 'fashion-forward' today means obsessing about a bag or shoe, but I'd like to make it fashion-forward to pay attention to the true cost of these harmful habits. Shop with our values forefront in our hearts and minds. We do not have to compromise beauty or style to do the right thing. Commit to buying better by making better shopping decisions.

How do you start?

Ask questions: it is imperative that our favourite brands know how important it is for us to know where our clothes and accessories are made and who made them. Ask the salespeople. Ask the CEOs. Ask the designers themselves. Push brands to be more responsible and accountable, both environmentally and socially. If we ask questions and make better choices when we buy, then brands will produce more responsible options for us to purchase. Let's use our stylish influence for good!

Change your buying habits

Choose timeless pieces and avoid seasonal trends. Timeless, classic, stunning: these are the qualities I look for when buying something new. There is nothing like a well-made piece with a great fit. These are the items that will be in my closet for years. We don't have to concede a love of fashion to wear clothes from brands that manufacture responsibly.

Fashion company Reformation designs and produces limited-edition collections at their factory in Los Angeles, and incorporates sustainable practices throughout its supply chain.

Model, actress and sustainable fashion mentor Amber Valletta transformed her shopping habits to buy better. (See her tips on p. 43).

Create a capsule wardrobe

Let's face it, we struggle to shut the doors of our overflowing wardrobes and still moan that we have nothing to wear. So what are our closets full of? Too often, our clothes don't match and are not easily styled together, making getting dressed time-consuming and frustrating, and adding further burdens to busy lives.

Creating a capsule wardrobe with a smaller number of staples that can be effortlessly worn together will pay big rewards in terms of time and effort, as you'll get more looks with fewer pieces that will reflect your own style better. Your clothes will also be of better quality and will, therefore, be more sustainable. Curating a capsule wardrobe could just mean a careful edit of clothes you already own, or you could apply the 'buy less, buy better' mantra to future purchasing. Either way, you'll end up with quality clothes that you will love and wear for years to come.

1

Less is more

A capsule wardrobe is all about making your closet manageable and stylish. This means limiting the clothes you own to versatile, high-quality items that can be worn in many different ways. Less is more: capsule wardrobes usually consist of around 20 to 30 pieces, including dresses, bottoms, tops and outerwear, although the final number will depend on your lifestyle. Those grappling with such minimalism can take comfort from the fact that it doesn't include underwear, sleepwear and workout gear. Once you've whittled down your wardrobe, stick to the rule that if something goes in, something else must come out.

2

Stay true to your style

You will get a lot of wear from your capsule wardrobe, so it pays to choose clothes that are comfortable and stylish, and complement your colouring, body shape and lifestyle. Draw inspiration from what you already own and wear, from magazines or blogs, or from a bit of people-watching (in the pursuit of research, of course!) This will allow you to create a mood board to print and carry with you, store on your phone or keep inside your head as you shop. Doing so will make it easier to choose pieces that complement the clothes you already own and you will be less likely to succumb to impulse buys, which only lead to regret and more wardrobe waste.

3

Build the backbone

You will need a few versatile basics to form the backbone of your capsule wardrobe, including jeans, T-shirts and sweaters. Allocate at least half of your capsule wardrobe allowance to basics, and then splash out on a couple of special pieces that will complement them. If you work in an office, then aim for 50 per cent of your capsule wardrobe to be work wear.

4

Consider colours and contours

One of the most important considerations in building a capsule wardrobe is to curate colours and silhouettes carefully. If all your colour tones complement one another, then your options become endless. For example, 20 garments can give you over 50 different outfit combinations or more, if you use bold accessories to transform outfits. Also remember that balance is key, as a good mix of fitted and loose clothing will take you through any number of social scenarios and climates.

5

Caring for your wardrobe

You will be wearing the items in your capsule wardrobe frequently, so they will need careful attention to manage the inevitable wear and tear. Choose clothes that can be easily washed and repaired. Jeans, for example, are versatile and durable – and, according to some, only need washing once a year! You may want to avoid very delicate fabrics that require dry cleaning, which is not only expensive and polluting, but also means that one or more items from your small wardrobe will be out of action during cleaning. (See chapter 3 for more about clothing care.)

6

Invest in the best

Your capsule wardrobe will work best when based on timeless looks, so it pays to invest in classic items such as a pair of quality jeans or a blazer. These may be more expensive, but be confident that because you are buying fewer pieces, you can extend your budget. Allow yourself to aim for special pieces that will reward you financially and fashionably over time. Think about price per wear, and this will help you dig deeper for better quality items, knowing you'll get your money's worth in the long run.

Dress for the seasons

You will need to adjust your capsule wardrobe throughout the year to reflect the seasons. Naturally, the extent of this will depend on how varied the seasonal changes are where you live. Try to find clothes that can transcend the seasons, such as tops that can be layered or a skirt that looks as good with bare legs as it does with tights.

Bring in the professionals

Stylists and personal shoppers are not just for the rich and famous. It may be worth investing in the services of a stylist, so that your capsule wardrobe gets off to its most stylish start. A professional can identify key garments that work for you and with the others in your wardrobe, giving you the confidence to invest in better pieces for the long term. Plus, experts can show you different styling options to give you more looks without added consumption.

TANIA REINERT-SHCHELKANOVTSEVA

Having discovered the truth about the dirty business of fashion through researching and writing her blog, Tania Reinert-Shchelkanovtseva decided to seek an alternative to meaningless consumption. After failing to find an online store that combined the ethics and aesthetics she was looking for, she co-founded the pioneering online eco-boutique A Boy Named Sue in 2012, along with business partner Samantha Wong.

'I used to shop to make myself feel better, pass the time or be on trend. But as I learned more about the dreadful impact of fast fashion, I realized I had to overhaul my buying habits. I donated all of those mediocre pieces I never wore and edited what was left down to perfect basics and unique, beautiful pieces. "Quality over quantity" has been my motto ever since.'

Tania's essentials for a capsule wardrobe

Quality trumps quantity

One high-quality merino wool sweater will last you many seasons, whereas fast-fashion garments will only last a few months, or even a few weeks.

Avoid trends

Think about what goes with what you already have. My golden rule is that if the piece doesn't go with anything you currently own, avoid it at all costs.

My staples

Two good pairs of jeans (grey and black); three T-shirts in grey, white and navy; silk tank tops in colours that suit you; one cream and one navy jumper; a good coat and a biker jacket; a few cool scarves; a pair of shorts that can be dressed up or down; a white suit jacket and a long dress that looks good with bare feet or a pair of heels; a beautiful statement piece; a chic and comfy pair of flats and a killer pair of heels. With these few items in your wardrobe, you are ready for anything.

Banker-turned-blogger Tania Reinert-Shchelkanovtseva co-founded A Boy Named Sue while on a mission to build a conscious capsule wardrobe. (See her tips on p. 53).

Employing a 100 per cent transparency policy, Honest by is the world's first fashion brand to share the full cost breakdown of its products – and profits – with customers.

Take action

Fashion is nothing without you, the consumer. Your money is to the fashion industry what water is to life on earth. It can't survive without it. This means that your purse, and how often you are willing to open it and what factors cause you to irreversibly snap it shut, is at the core of the business of clothes.

Each time you spend your money, you are casting your vote for what you believe in. But it's not just your cash that does the talking: another powerful tool at your disposal is the simple art of making your voice heard. Speaking up to friends, family and fashion brands will inspire small ripples of change. If you're inspired to act, you will need to take control of your purse strings. Doing so will liberate you, so that you can become your own gorgeously stylish, modern-day fashion activist.

1

Exert your purse-power

The retail giants didn't get to the size they are today without our cash to fuel them. What's stocked in-store is ultimately determined by what consumers want to buy, and your purse-power can influence the success or demise of the clothes ranges available. To maximize this power, search for a few stylish brands that have well-documented environmentally and socially sustainable practices, and remain loyal. Your shopping experience will be more streamlined, and you'll be rewarding those brands with the integrity you value with the money they need to grow.

2

Speak up

Make your voice heard! Send an email or a letter, fill in a comments card or speak to the staff in-store. If you can't find garments made from organic, Fairtrade or recycled cotton in your favourite shop, or if you want information about where your clothes were made to be more readily available, ring the head office to let them know you'll be taking your business elsewhere unless you get the answers you need. Ask what the company's environmental and social policies are, and why more sustainable products aren't available. You may not get all the answers, but your questions might trigger discussions within the company. If the customer is always right, then speaking up collectively will put these issues at the top of the boardroom agenda.

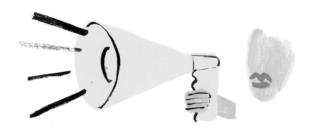

3

Use social media

Don't underestimate your power to influence: share your experiences and opinions with your social network. Brands are rightly sensitive about how their customers – their very lifeline – talk about their products. You can be an inspiration simply by sharing with your friends what you have learned and by showing your support for sustainable brands and initiatives by liking, re-tweeting and sharing these with your social circle. Become a fashion activist by alerting your friends to what you've discovered about a brand's production processes.

Take a stand

Show your support by signing petitions, joining campaigns or going to live events. Increasingly, there are powerful initiatives receiving widespread consumer support that are driving media awareness – and boardroom attention. Pledging commitment to an issue can also connect you with others who share your views, and taking part in campaigns, from spending a day without shoes to wearing your clothes inside out, can be an eye-opening experience. Search online for campaigns, such as Greenpeace and Fashion Revolution, which cover issues close to your heart, and never underestimate your power to influence.

Consider your consumer care

As consumers, we can feel like a small, lone voice in the wilderness raised against one of the world's largest industries, which, after all, dresses over seven billion people. But there are ways to get yourself heard and get more hands-on with the issues at the same time. Consider donating your time and expertise, even money, to organizations that are working towards improving the fashion industry's environmental and social impacts. You can channel your support to a group that needs a helping hand, and ultimately contribute to a bigger mission.

ORSOLA DE CASTRO

Fashion designer and campaigner Orsola de Castro is the founder of upcycling label From Somewhere, and the co-founder of both Estethica, a British Fashion Council initiative at London Fashion Week 2006–14, and Fashion Revolution, an international coalition of academics, designers and organizations who are demanding increased transparency in the fashion supply chain.

'Too many stories have been told, harrowing images seen, and information about polluted rivers and widespread malpractice reported in the global press for consumers not to be aware of these issues. And those that were aware of this state of affairs all along are now more outspoken in demanding change. The message is spreading, and the consumer is beginning to ask relevant and more meaningful questions about how the fashion industry operates.'

Orsola's essentials for taking action

Become part of the solution

Don't feel as if you have inherited a massive problem. Start with small changes, make a personal pledge and discover what works for you. Think of sustainability as being about more choice, rather than less: more creativity, more thinking, more empowerment.

Ask more questions

We must put pressure on big business to solve the problems and suffering around the world. If you don't know how or where your clothes are made, it is essential that you find out and demand the information from the brands you buy from. Support more sustainably created products, and wear them proudly as a reflection of your true inner self.

Join the revolution

Anyone, regardless of profession, can raise awareness and inspire others to stand up, speak up and take part in a consumer revolution. Use the power of social media to engage with others, because even the simplest online post can have a ripple effect.

Designer Orsola de Castro is as active in spreading a consumer revolution as she is designing clothes, and believes that the issue of transparency is at the heart of effecting change. (See her tips on p. 63).

SOKO Kenya produces a sustainable fashion range for ASOS, which supports local business by nurturing craftsmanship (top). Jeans by Korra are sewn by a single tailor in India, who signs each finished pair (bottom).

Wear

The reality

These bad clothing habits result in a huge waste of our own money and the earth's natural resources. Our disconnection with the clothes we wear and inability to manage them can make getting dressed feel overwhelming on a busy morning. So it's no surprise that the state of our wardrobes can seem as if it is in as much of a crisis as the environment.

I f it's true that you are what you wear, then today's closets speak of chaos and crisis. Inside our overfull wardrobes lies the proof of our unsustainable clothing consumption patterns and attitudes. We buy far too many clothes, and then rarely wear them to their full potential.

This also means that we're in the dark about the clothes we already own. We're more likely to know what's in our fridge than in our closet, meaning that we're missing out on the fashion potential staring out at us from the racks, shelves and drawers of clothes that fill our homes.

'If you can commit to wearing something 30 times, it's already fantastic, no matter where you bought it. I buy with purpose and have things I wear over and over again.'
Livia Firth, Eco-Age

Here's what you need to know...

We under-wear our clothes

It's estimated that we only wear 20 per cent of our clothes 80 per cent of the time.[14] This means that while we stick to our habitual default mode of wearing the same outfits over and over again, our closets are bursting with untapped fashion potential.

We don't wear the clothes we buy

Studies show that 58 per cent of people in the UK aged 16 to 24 have unworn clothes in their closets that no longer suit their style or taste. This situation is accelerated by today's fast-paced fashion trends, which can make even newly purchased clothes feel outdated as soon as the hangtags have been removed.[16]

Our clothes don't fit

Approximately 85 per cent of women in the UK own clothes that don't fit them, usually because we hang onto favourite items even after, over the years, our body shape has changed.[15] Many of these ill-fitting clothes could be ushered back into fashion service with the help of a needle and thread – or the resourceful know-how of a good tailor.

We hang onto clothes

Around 30 per cent of the clothes hanging in UK wardrobes haven't been worn for at least 12 months – a figure that represents a staggering £30 billion worth of unused garments.[17] Our failure to sort out and pass on unworn clothing has the effect of locking away both money and natural resources within the confines of our closets.

Things you can do

But you can make easy changes to reduce your impact on the environment and maximize the style and appeal of your clothes. The first step in having a more conscious closet is facing up to the reality that we have plenty of clothes we do not make use of responsibly. Next, we need to manage our clothing inventory effectively, which requires some commitment. Whenever you feel like revamping your style, whether because of changes in lifestyle or in taste, you'll also need to invest time, honesty and generosity in releasing your clothes, so that they can live on elsewhere, instead of languishing unworn at the back of your wardrobe.

If you are indeed what you wear, then now is the time to act accordingly, so that your clothes reflect the real you. Be inspired to edit your closet, and, with a little DIY, restyle, tailor and redesign your clothes, all of which will give you the most wear from your wardrobe without wear and tear on the environment. Getting dressed in the morning will never be the same.

Edit your closet

We tend to keep clothes for the wrong reasons, waiting for the rainy day when we'll be two sizes smaller or 10 years younger. The resulting crammed, chaotic closets make it challenging for anyone, even the most battle-hardened fashionistas, to get dressed. Disorganized wardrobes are more likely to send you straight to the shops, rather than encouraging you to discover and wear the clothes you already have.

By contrast, a well-organized and edited wardrobe will reward you with the most efficient use of its valuable contents. You'll reap the financial, environmental and fashion rewards stored behind its doors – if, that is, you can actually see what you've already bought. So when editing and reorganizing, think 'boutique', rather than 'jumble sale', and you'll find yourself wanting to 'shop' from your own closet every morning.

Don't cut corners

Your wardrobe review needs time – three hours, minimum – to give it the attention it deserves. As with most things, rushing leads to cutting corners in your decision-making process, and you may find yourself keeping or disposing of clothes for the wrong reasons. Ask a friend to help you – a truthful, rather than kind, friend is best – to make journeying into the furthest reaches of your wardrobe easier and more enjoyable. To keep things under control, try to do a closet edit every six months.

Let the skeletons out

To take full stock of the situation, you will need to empty your entire wardrobe and lay it all out in one place, including any clothes that have found their way into extra cupboards, the loft or the garage. Assessing all of your clothes in one go will help you rediscover forgotten items and identify repeated purchases in similar colours and styles (how many pairs of black trousers do you own? Or need?) And lastly, you'll be better able to spot new outfit combinations.

3

Scrutinize your clothes

Once everything is laid out and you've recovered from seeing just how much it is that you own, start scrutinizing. Try on all of your clothes in front of a full-length mirror to remind yourself what you like about them. It's no good reviewing clothes while they're on hangers, because – unlike the sometimes painful experience of viewing your trouser-clad backside in a mirror – clothes that are just hanging up in a wardrobe can be misleading. Ask yourself if you love the item, and if it fits. Have you worn it recently? Would you buy it again if you saw it in the shop today? Put your clothes into two piles: 'yes' and 'no'. Be honest with yourself, otherwise you'll end up returning everything back to the wardrobe.

4

Tackle the 'no' pile

Next, go through your 'no' pile to get to the bottom of what you're not wearing and why. Don't be in a rush to discard. Think about ways to give the clothes new life: do they need stain treatment or repair, for example. Then split the 'no' pile into smaller piles: those items needing care and attention or repair (see chapter 3 for more on clothing care); restyling (pp. 82–5); redesigning (pp. 100–7) or disposal (see chapter 4). But be strict: temper those fantasies about attending endless balls and banquets or shifting that last 10 kg (22 lbs), so that you don't put anything back into your closet you probably won't wear.

5

Sort the 'yes' pile

Now, back to the 'yes' pile, with which you will restock your closet. First, group garment types (trousers, skirts, tops) together, and then organize by colour. Be thorough when restocking: a highly organized wardrobe will pay back dividends as you become inspired by new, previously unimagined outfit combinations. Your stylish boutique-like closet will beckon you out of bed in the morning, so that dressing becomes a pleasure, rather than a pain.

6

Divide and conquer

You may want to split up what's left of your clothes into seasons, so that your daily outfit edit is even quicker. Access is key in ensuring you wear your wardrobe to its maximum, so storage will become an important part of your closet edit, allowing you more room for inspired dressing (see pp. 166–71 for more about storage).

Document it

If you want to take your wardrobe edit even further (think Cher's epic computerized walk-in closet in the film *Clueless*), make lists, take photos, label your clothes or use one of the many apps out there, such as Stylebook or KonMari. Documenting what you own helps both the sorting process and efficient use for the future by ensuring your wardrobe's contents are quick to view. This system works especially well for shoeboxes and garment bags, where contents aren't always visible.

Go with a pro

Finally, if the idea of editing your closet feels overwhelming, you could always bring in the experts. You don't need a celebrity wardrobe or bank balance to do this. Investing in a one-off wardrobe edit with a stylist or closet organizer will make sense of your clothes and bring them back into fashion action. You're also likely to get some great advice on outfit combinations along the way. Find someone who matches your style and understands body shapes. These days, you can even do it online.

GRETA EAGAN

US-based stylist and make-up artist Greta Eagan is the author of *Wear No Evil: How to Change the World with Your Wardrobe*, and writes the popular eco-chic blog Fashion Me Green. She also contributes to publications such as *Tank* magazine and the Huffington Post, and has worked on brand collaborations with the likes of *Glamour*, Kate Spade, Eileen Fisher and The Outnet.

'I love a good closet edit and usually set aside a full afternoon to devote to it. I'll also recruit a friend to help give the "yea" or "nay" on items.'

Greta's essentials for a closet edit

Dress seasonally
By rotating my clothes with the seasons, my wardrobe feels less cluttered. Plus, only the clothes that are suitable for the current season are visible. This means that putting outfits together and getting dressed in the morning is easier. You can store out-of-season clothes in a container, and when the time comes to pull them out again, you'll feel like you've got a whole new wardrobe!

Keep what makes you happy
When having a clearout, hold the item in your hand and ask if it brings you joy. If the answer is an instant 'yes', then you know you should keep it. But if you begin by telling yourself that it was a gift, how expensive it was or how it might suit you one day, then you should probably let it go. I was taught this by organizing expert Marie Kondo and love how simple and effective it is.

Organize what's left
When putting your 'yes' clothes back in the closet, organize them by type and colour. I hang my shirts together, then skirts, sweaters, and so on. Then I group similar colours to create a clothing rainbow (white, beige, pink, purple, orange, green, blue, grey, black, brown), making it easier when getting dressed to choose pieces that complement the overall look.

Greta Eagan keeps her closet in order with regular clearouts, which help her to identify new outfits and combinations with ease. (See her tips on p. 79).

'A piece of clothing is also just a configuration of fabric that can be manipulated on the body. Layering differently can alter outfits entirely.' – Susie Lau, fashion writer and editor

Restyle it

It's a common scene and one we've all witnessed – and even starred in. Woman stands in front of her overflowing closet and exclaims: 'I have nothing to wear!' The reality is that most of us have more clothes than we need. This misconception occurs when we let convenience dictate our style and reach for the same old clothing combinations, rather than let the amount of choice excite or interest us.

But rather than overhauling your wardrobe or going on a shopping spree, you could instead release your inner stylist and give your existing clothes a fresh lease of life simply by restyling and accessorizing them. Stepping outside of your fashion comfort zone and expanding your style will leave you with many 'new' outfits, without the need to visit the shops or create more fashion waste.

'For different styling combinations, cardigans can be worn as skirts if buttoned up and tied around the hips. Long skirts can be shifted up to become dresses. Jackets and coats can be draped on the shoulders or tightened with belts to create different silhouettes.'

Susie Lau, fashion writer and editor

1

Find inspiration everywhere

Having completed your closet edit and discovered long-forgotten items lurking at the back of the wardrobe, no doubt you have lots of ideas. Get even more by studying style magazines, reading blogs and people-watching. Adapt aspects of the style of people you admire. Have a look, too, at the many online tutorials out there, which provide styling advice according to body shape, skin tone and lifestyle.

2

Maximize your options

We are all guilty of falling into the trap of wearing the same items of clothing in the same combinations. Try experimenting with different styling options: tucking a shirt in or wearing it loose, tied at the front or rolled up at the sleeves, or rolling up your jeans or pinning up a hem for the day. And don't be limited by an item's original use: try wearing your dress as a skirt or as a top. Layering allows you to create new outfits while playing around with proportions. Try wearing a shirt under a strapless dress to make it work- (and winter-) appropriate, or add tights to your shorts to wear them through the seasons. You'll be surprised at how many outfits you can create.

Mix it up

Combine prints and colours to
create an individualized look. A dash
of pattern, even better if daringly
clashed, makes your wardrobe stand
out and go further. Try combining two
patterns in the same colour scheme,
or mixing a large-scale print with
a smaller scale one.

Capture the results

With all this experimental styling
going on, why not photograph the
results and build your own personal
'look book' to catalogue the different
combinations? Just imagine how quick
dressing in the morning will become!
If you want to take the documenting
process one step further, check out the
wardrobe apps available to help you
categorize and document your clothes.

Accessorize to maximize

Changing accessories and shoes is
the easiest way to transform an outfit.
Heels or flats give a dress an entirely
different look; a statement necklace
with a crisp, white shirt adds zing; a
standout scarf worn over a T-shirt ups
the style factor. The key to successful
accessorizing, taking you from work
to a night out, is to have good-quality
staples and statement pieces – belts,
necklaces, tights, shoes – in different
colours and sizes, as these will help
your closet go further.

Tailor it

Most wardrobes contain clothes that will never fit properly without the expert hand of a tailor – a situation that is not entirely of our own making. Today's clothes, ranging from mass-produced to well-made investment pieces, are cut to just eight to ten standard body sizes, which differ from brand to brand. So unless you're a cookie-cutter copy of a particular brand's fitting model, your clothes will not fit perfectly.

Although we tend to shy away from using a tailor – partly because today's cheaper clothes feel at odds with the costs associated with custom alterations – a well-fitting wardrobe needs a tailor's expertise. So embrace your tailor: he or she will give you the fit and feel of couture at a fraction of the cost. The better an item of clothing fits, the better you will look and feel, and the more you will wear it. Include tailoring as an integral part of your wardrobe repertoire, and you'll show off not just your more sustainable approach to fashion, but also your best curves, too.

Find the fit

First, you need to know what fits you. Get dressed in front of a mirror (and possibly an honest friend), and look for where hemlines sit in relation to your waistline. Check if the waistline itself is too tight (pinching around the midriff) or too loose (drooping or baggy garments that hide your shape), and that your jackets don't swamp your shoulders or cut off circulation at your armpits. Once you've identified poorly fitting areas, experiment using pins and clips to see how you could improve the fit through small alterations, before deciding what needs tailoring.

Examine your tailoring pile

Next, scrutinize the pile of clothes destined for alteration and decide if they're worth the money. Will you wear this item more if it fits perfectly? Is it made of good-quality fabric? Think about how much the alterations are likely to cost. As a general rule, the easiest (and cheapest) alterations to make are where there is already a seam in place, such as hems. If you want to make an item bigger, check that there is enough seam allowance. Altering clothes with linings is more complicated, as is lowering or raising waistlines or narrowing shoulders in jackets. Thicker and more robust fabrics, such as wool and denim, are easier to alter than silk and velvet. As a general guide, a simple alteration can run to about £10 ($13), and a suit alteration from £40–50 ($52–65) on up, depending on the tailor and the task.

Find a good tailor

Finding the right tailor is important, particularly if you're entrusting him or her with a cherished family item. Avoid going straight to the nearest or cheapest tailor, and instead ask for recommendations, search online for reviews and check examples of any prospective tailor's work. Compare prices and quality, as these vary enormously, but don't be guided by price alone: some excellent tailors work in the cheapest shops around. Finally, some department stores and shops have in-house tailors, so you shouldn't have to go far to find one.

Discuss your requirements

Once you've found your tailor, ask for their advice. Talk your ideas and the process through before they make a single cut. Unless you're doing a simple seam or strap adjustment, ask for a fitting as this will give you the best results. If this is your first time using a tailor, or you're not sure about your garment's ideal fit, don't worry. A good tailor will know what's wrong with the fit and, more importantly, how to fix it for you.

Do it yourself

If the cost of a tailor is too much, or the garment isn't worth the investment, try going it alone. Keep to simple adjustments, such as hems or seams, and search online for sewing tutorials, both for inspiration and for step-by-step guides. YouTube is a great resource, or you could go further and sign up for a local course.

'Good tailoring is just one way of ensuring that my clothes work harder for me. Like me, women today want clothes that fit perfectly. Going to a tailor means that they look better, feel better and last longer.'

Erin Mullaney, fashion and retail consultant

DIY it

We are all familiar with the feeling of disappointment we get when a favourite item of clothing becomes outdated, stained, worn out or just doesn't fit anymore. On first inspection, such offenders may appear destined for the bin, despite the cash we shelled out for them and their sentimental value.

This is where DIY fashion – the fashionista's answer to home improvement – can save the day, or at least the garment. Fashion fans have much to rave about: you can create new from old, while creating one-of-a-kind looks that help you stand out from the crowd. It can be cheap, if not free, and can give a high-fashion look without costing the earth. Finally, you can revel in the satisfaction of making something yourself while reusing valuable resources and rescuing special clothes from potential ruin.

'DIY is the perfect way to put your own stamp on style. You can take a popular trend and create your own version, giving you a unique look while spending less.'
Jenni Radosevich, I Spy DIY

Take your time

Rushing a project can prove disastrous to both the outcome and your nerves. Worse still, a rushed job risks ruining the garment with poorly thought-out scissor-cuts, leaving you with a piece of clothing that's worse off than when you started. So take your time and think it through before trying out new techniques. Whether making simple cuts here or adding intricate beading there, DIY does have something for everyone. And you don't even need sewing skills: some projects require only a glue gun and a dash of bravery.

Review your candidates

You may already have a pile of unusable clothes from your closet edit (see pp. 72–7), or you'll have to scour your wardrobe for likely contenders. Once you've done so, set about identifying each garment's positive features. Do you love the print but not the shape? Do you like the style but not the colour? Does it have sentimental value but is a poor fit? Is the garment made from quality fabrics but feels outdated? Is it only partially stained? The answers to these questions will help guide the nature and complexity of your DIY project.

3

Have a clear vision

With your DIY candidates identified, you'll need to have a clear vision of the desired outcome. Stay realistic: start out small for your first few projects, until you grow in confidence. Take your cue from fashion magazines, blogs and what other people are wearing, and then visualize how the garment will look and function when it is completed. Take into account the seasons and your lifestyle to avoid creating something you'll never wear. If you need help, there are plenty of blogs, including I Spy DIY and Geneva Vanderzeil's A Pair & A Spare (see pp. 96–9), books and video tutorials that give step-by-step guidance. But don't pressure yourself into replicating what someone else has done: fashion is fun and experimental, and DIY should be, too!

4

Gather your tools

You'll need a basic toolkit. A decent pair of scissors, needles, thread, some glue and various shades of dye are the minimum required to resuscitate your clothes. Next are the fun frills, like buttons, lace, scraps of fabric and sequins. Before rushing out to buy new, scour your home for these. You'll be surprised at what you find. A broken necklace can be taken apart for use as beading, and lace from an old dress or tablecloth can be turned into trimming. Ask your family and friends for their unwanted ribbons, buttons and thread – or whole sewing kits. Finally, turn to a haberdashery or online shop as a last resort once you've gathered up all the readily available and free materials you can get your hands on.

5

Choose your fabrics

Get to know the fabrics you'll be working with. If you're a beginner, start with cotton or polyester, as these are more forgiving to the untrained hand. Some fabrics, such as silk and lace, are more difficult to sew, because they tend to be slippery or can pucker as you work. Thicker materials like leather or denim can be tricky for beginners, as they are tougher to get a needle through. But as always, perseverance and the right tools will pay off, and you should be able to power your way through most fabrics. To build confidence, practise on scraps before moving on to the real thing.

6

Consider clothing care

Think about how you'll care for the finished item once you've completed your project. You don't want your 'new' garment to have a complicated life in your laundry basket or a purposeless one in your closet. Think twice before combining delicate and tough fabrics, as silk and denim need different treatments during washing. Adding sequins makes washing a bit more difficult, as can combining different colours that can't be washed together. Will you be able to easily wash that electric blue trim on your otherwise white dress? (See chapter 3 for more on clothing care.)

Control your cuts

In different hands, scissors can be either a garment's friend or foe. But with careful cutting, even in the hands of an inexperienced DIYer, a pair of scissors can transform an outfit. Take a garment from frumpy to fashion-forward by simply cutting off long sleeves or shortening hemlines, or transform a trench coat into a cropped jacket or a torn pair of jeans into hot pants – all without the need to hit the shops. The golden rule, as ever, is to measure twice and cut once. And make sure you have decent sewing shears that will slice crisply through fabric, rather than ordinary household scissors that will butcher it. When it comes to scissors, you really can blame a bad project on your tools.

Upcycle with trimmings

Adding beads, lace, studs, transfers or patches is a stress-free way to upcycle an old garment. It is also particularly good for disguising stains or areas with irreparable damage. Transform a plain top by adding beads or studs, resuscitate an old jacket by changing its length or adding patterned patch pockets, or drag old clothes into this century simply by changing the buttons or adding a sequinned trim. Effective, cheap and easy!

9

Let dyes loose

Dyeing is another quick way to salvage a worn-out or faded garment that has lost a little sparkle. If you're feeling particularly creative, add a unique twist through dip-dyeing or tie-dyeing, but remember to opt for environmentally friendly dyes. Some natural dyes – from beetroot to turmeric – can even be found in your kitchen. If you're going down the natural dye route, you will need to chop the plant material, add water and then heat to release the colour. Then fix the colour into the fabric with salt (for berry-based dyes) or white-wine vinegar (for plant-based dyes), so the colours don't wash out. Check online for tutorials.

10

A good finish is key

The final finish determines where in the fashion stakes your DIY project will sit. So always take extra time over your finishing stitches to ensure your garment looks more couture than craft. The devil is in the detail!

GENEVA VANDERZEIL

Hong Kong and Australia-based writer Geneva Vanderzeil originally intended her blog A Pair & A Spare to be a place to record her lifelong passion for DIY fashion. Over time, it has expanded to become a hugely successful lifestyle site, where she shares DIY tutorials, fashion ideas, travel tips and business advice. When not creating catwalk-worthy creations from thrift-shop buys or appearing on television, Geneva collaborates with brands that include Coach, Marriot and Visa. She is also the author of *DIY Fashionista*.

'I am a huge fan of using creative approaches to revitalize fashion items so they can be reused. DIY is a great way to inject some individuality and create outfits that carry your memories and personality. It's also a good way to look stylish, while being conscious of the environment at the same time.'

Geneva's DIY essentials

Find inspiration everywhere

I'm always studying fashion magazines, catwalk collections and street looks, as these inspire me when thinking about what to do with my own clothes. Gathering ideas in this way allows you to look fashionable without buying anything new or breaking the bank.

Focus on the finish

My top DIY tip is to focus on the finish. A tidy and well-stitched (or glued) garment will ensure that the result looks more haute couture than high street. Pay particular attention to hemlines and any rough edges, and practise patience and attention to detail as you near the finishing line.

Add embellishments

A great DIY starting point, because it's the simplest way to produce maximum impact. You can completely transform an item simply by adding studs, beads, lace – anything you want. Plus, it's fun!

For Geneva's rhinestone bomber jacket, you will need
a round-necked sweatshirt; rhinestones; glue; scissors; needle and thread.
Mark the centre of the sweatshirt with a chalk pencil and cut down the middle.

Once you have pinned the cut edges and sewn them, either by hand or with
a machine, get creative and arrange your rhinestone pattern before gluing it down.
The finished article! (See more of Geneva's tips on p. 97).

Redesign it

Sometimes we have clothes that can't be brought back to life by taking up a hem or adding a row of beading. These could be cherished investment pieces or family hand-me-downs, which need more serious attention to get them back into action.

In these situations, the skills of a tailor alone won't solve the problem. Redesigning, either on your own or with the help of a fashion designer, allows you to rethink, recreate and transform your clothes. It also involves some pretty major (sometimes irreversible) steps, however, so it's best reserved for when you are absolutely sure, because the final cut really is just that.

'I've loved working with my trusted seamstress over the years to redesign favourite pieces into showstopping performance outfits. I treat it as an art form.'
Sandy Lam, singer

Identify suitable candidates

Look through your closet to find clothes that are ready for the redesign treatment. These shouldn't be hard to identify, as they will generally be items of sentimental value or made from exquisite fabrics or prints. Ask yourself what you like about the garment, and if it is made from a high-quality material. Would you wear it more if it was a different style? The lace from your bridesmaid's dress, the print used for your mother's shirt or your granny's crochet work could all be the perfect starting point for a new, more wearable item.

Collect ideas

Get inspiration from magazines and blogs, and go for style over trends, as this will ensure your redesigned garment does not itself become outdated. Think of what new items you could create, and don't be limited by the garment's original purpose. Who said your grandmother's ballgown can't become a stunning top, or a charity-shop find can't look exquisitely high-fashion? Have a clear idea of what you want before making the first cut, or call on a fashion designer for advice.

3

Go it alone ...

If you have the technical skills to do the redesigning yourself, make sure you plan the process thoroughly before picking up the scissors. Working with used garments isn't the same as working with fresh rolls of fabric. Once an item of clothing is deconstructed, it will still bear the traces of old cuts and seams. Depending on the piece, you may also need to address or work around any stains or damage (see chapter 3 for more about clothing care). But don't be daunted: even damage can be turned from a fault into a feature. If you need more guidance, look for patterns online, ask in your local haberdashery shop or sign up for a sewing class, which has the added bonus of giving you new skills and perhaps a new hobby.

... or call in the experts

There are more and more designers out there who specialize in transforming clothes into runway-ready designs. How you find your designer will vary depending on where you live. Look up local studios or go online and search for bespoke reconstruction, recycling or upcycling fashion specialists. Check out emerging designers at your nearest fashion-design college: they will have the skills and may want to build up their experience (and bank balance). If you've got a very strong vision in mind, however, you may want to choose a seamstress, rather than a designer or design student, to avoid any possible creative clashes.

JOHANNA HO

Fashion designer Johanna Ho has a passion for sustainable design, from reconstruction to zero-waste. Following studies at Central Saint Martins, she showed her inaugural collection at London Fashion Week, and her work has sold at Browns, Selfridges and Harrods in London and Harvey Nichols and Liger in Hong Kong, in addition to her own e-shop. Johanna has collaborated with Vans, Birkenstock and Lane Crawford, and her celebrity following includes actresses Gwyneth Paltrow, Lana Del Rey, Hilary Tsui and Eason Chan.

'Don't think of your unwanted clothes as a precursor to waste. If you work with fashion designers, who have the creativity to reinvent your clothes in unexpected ways, you'll find that previously unwanted garments become coveted pieces. I've been reconstructing my friends' clothes for years by transforming them into outfits that they love and wear, from onstage at concerts to the front row at catwalks.'

Johanna's essentials for redesigning

Not all clothes are worth saving

Start by assessing the value of your unwanted clothes and consider whether or not they are worth the effort. Those that are have value, both financial and emotional, so think about high-quality fabrics and clothes with sentimental associations.

Visualize its new purpose

Do you want a skirt but have a dress, or do you want culottes but have a skirt? If you can get a rough idea of the shape, style and function of your prospective garment, you can give your designer some direction, enabling them to create something you will love and cherish for years to come.

Match designer to budget

There are many designers out there with a talent for reconstructing who are looking for creative work. So don't feel that working with a fashion designer is only for the rich and famous! With a little thought and research, you'll find that it's much more accessible than that. Try searching online or on local community boards for 'custom made', 'reconstructed' or 'personalized' clothing in your area, or get in touch with your local fashion college to meet designers who are just starting out.

Fashion designer Johanna Ho is a pro at redesigning unwanted garments into 'new' outfits, letting her imagination loose on seemingly castaway clothes. (See her tips on p. 105).

Katie Jones's eponymous knitwear label teams playful aesthetics with serious ethics. She and her team (which includes her mum) produce her designs by using designer surplus textiles.

Care

The reality

Gradually, and perhaps unwittingly, we've moved away from carefully looking after our clothes and towards quick disposal, a decline matched by a rise in consumerism. Buying new now trumps caring for old. Consequently, skills such as cleaning, sewing and storing are fading out of fashion and many of us can't thread a needle, let alone know where to find one.

Not only are we caring less for our clothes, we are also damaging them – or worse – during our everyday cleaning routines. In the quest for convenience, speed and perfection, we tend to reach for the hamper instead of the hanger. Many of us now habitually over-wash our clothes, prematurely aging them by boiling, bleaching and tumbling them in the washing machine and dryer to remove the odd whiff or minor stain.

With our washing machines in constant use, guzzling energy and churning out soapsuds, we are damaging both the environment and our clothes – which we then transfer from the washing machine to the tumble dryer without a second thought, removing fibres as well as water during the drying process. Where do you think all that fluff in the filter comes from? And then there are the dry cleaners, who dip clothes into vats of toxic liquid chemicals. There's nothing dry about it!

This downturn in knowing how to care for our clothes, from washing errors to not staying on top of easy repairs, means that they fall out of the fashion loop too early. The failure to prevent or address damage causes problems that go beyond the offending item: it affects the environment and the people around us. As we send our clothes into early retirement, we perpetuate the production and over-consumption of new ones. Not caring for them means that landfills get ever fuller, natural resources drain away and pollutants are pumped continuously into waterways and ecosystems.

When it comes to caring for your clothes – and the environment – how you look after them really does matter.

Here's what you need to know...

How we wash has an impact
Between 75 and 80 per cent of our clothing's environmental impact during its entire life cycle – from processing the fibres and producing the fabric, all the way to the garment being worn, washed and then discarded – comes from washing and drying alone.[18]

We waste water and energy
We're a generation of clean freaks, with the average American family, according to one study, doing six loads of laundry per week.[20] But washing clothes uses lots of water and energy. In a typical household, laundry represents up to 20 per cent of all indoor water usage. Washing machines are energy-intense, with 90 per cent of that energy dedicated to heating the water. If everyone in the UK washed their clothes 10 per cent less, there would be a 2.6 per cent reduction in the UK's CO_2 emissions.

Washing damages our clothes
A survey of British consumers found that 10 per cent of respondents don't wear a particular garment because of stains or fading, or because it has become misshapen or has shrunk during washing.[19] As a result, millions of articles of clothing are retired before their time.

We pollute with chemicals
Many laundry detergents and fabric softeners are made from an extensive list of chemicals with tongue-twisting names like sodium lauryl sulfate (SLS) – and they are just as scary as they sound.[21] These chemicals get flushed away with the wastewater into our waterways and linger in our clothes, meaning that they are in contact with our skin.

Dry cleaning is toxic

Traditional dry cleaning has a significant environmental impact, and can also damage our clothes along the way. The most commonly used chemical in dry cleaning, perchloroethylene (perc), is known to have a negative environmental impact, as well as associated health risks.[22]

We don't mend our clothes

Getting out a needle and thread to sew on a button or fix a hem seems to be a thing of the past. One survey revealed that nearly one-third of UK respondents would bring more unused items of clothing back into use if they had the skills or time to repair them.[23] Millions of garments languish unworn at the back of our closets.

Things you can do

But protecting and caring for our clothes isn't always straightforward. Supermarkets are stocked with row upon row of detergents, each promising to remove stains better than the last, with little thought for the effect they have on the environment. Our clothes also seem to come in as many fabric types, each with different care instructions, as there are colours. Compounding this confusing scenario, many clothes produced today also suffer from a lack of quality and need all the care they can get.

Regardless of how well informed you are about clothing care, embracing better habits, from mending to storage, will reap rewards. Your clothes will be in active fashion service for longer, and your money won't be wasted by sending perfectly good items to landfill. With increased clothing-care confidence, you will know to invest in better-quality pieces and be confident that you'll be able to maintain them and get your money's worth. Better care will also make your environmental halo shine all the brighter to reflect your ever-more sustainable style.

Read on for tips on how to get to grips with better care habits, including how to wash, store and repair the items in your wardrobe, which will both save money and keep your clothes in tip-top fashion condition for years to come.

Getting to grips with clothing care

Whether you are a supermodel or a scientist, we are all faced with clothing that can occasionally be stained, wrinkled, torn, even smelly. The lack of skills and interest in caring for our clothes properly means that too often we buy new instead of reviving old. Having an understanding of the basic care options will protect your clothes and keep them working stylishly for you for longer. You will also be rewarded with a more conscious closet, as you save time, money and the planet.

'I've dedicated my career to championing more sustainable and beautiful textiles, and it breaks my heart when they are damaged through bad care. We must look after them, otherwise all of our efforts to protect the earth by producing these wonderful fabrics will be effectively washed down the plug hole.'
Giusy Bettoni, CEO and founder, C.L.A.S.S.

Know your fibres

Our clothes are made from many different kinds of fibres, each one of which likes to be treated differently. Begin by checking the labels: natural fibres such as wool and silk need more sensitive care, while synthetic fibres like polyester and nylon tend to be more robust. Then there are blended fibres, including stretchy, synthetic Lycra, which is added to cotton to produce that much-loved, sometimes much-needed, support, and cotton to which silk has been added for a touch of luxe. For garments made from blended fibres, follow the care instructions for the most delicate fibre in the mix.

Study the symbols

The most basic rule of garment care is to check the instructions on the label before you do anything else. Inserted by the manufacturer, these are based on the garment's specific fibre type to help prolong its lifespan. It isn't rocket science: the symbols cover how to wash, dry, iron and, in some cases, repair and dispose of your clothes. Some brands, however, can be overly cautious in their care instructions, sending you to the dry cleaners when handwashing or using the delicates cycle of the washing machine would do the job just as well in a more environmentally responsible, less costly way. But take comfort from the fact that your care labels are there to help, not hinder, in making your clothes last longer.

Know what needs extra care

Some fabrics require extra TLC. Knits and swimwear, for example, last longer when handwashed or put through the delicates cycle of the washing machine. Sequinned and embellished garments are best washed inside a laundry bag, which will give them an extra layer of protection and ensure they don't catch on other items in the drum. Towels, on the other hand, don't like fabric softeners as they reduce absorbency, so skip it to keep them in service for longer.

Rethink dry cleaning

There is a huge lack of knowledge about what goes on inside the dry cleaners. Yes, it's expensive, but it's also a chemically toxic process. Some of the chemicals used, most notably perchloroethylene, are linked to a frightening list of health issues, so it's no surprise that this killer chemical is bad for the environment, too. But armed with a solid understanding of fibres, you can substitute dry cleaning for a high-quality washing machine with a good range of programmes, or just roll your sleeves up and do your washing by hand. Items made from cashmere, wool and silk can be machine-washed in cold water or by hand, and then dried flat. If you must dry clean (coats or jackets, for example), opt for one of the growing family of environmentally conscious dry cleaners that use carbon-dioxide solvents or other non-toxic alternatives.

Ask questions

If you entrust a launderette or dry cleaner to do your cleaning for you, find out as much as you can about what happens to your clothes behind closed doors. Ask what machines are used and at which temperatures, and if the detergents used are safe for both people and the environment. You'll understand your clothing's impact more, and could trigger better cleaning methods around you. Finally, if you don't get the answers you want, take your business, and your dirty clothes, elsewhere.

'Having compiled a wardrobe of beautiful clothes that need to be looked after, I switched to an eco-friendly dry cleaner near me that uses biodegradable, health-friendly detergents. Everything comes back pristine, and it feels good that cleanliness hasn't been at the expense of the environment.'

Sarah Harris, Fashion Features Director, British Vogue

Safe stain removal

Stains are your clothes' most persistent enemy. Coffee, ketchup or dirt can ruin a favourite top or dress in a split second, with our own blood and sweat added to the mix. Without fast, effective treatment, stains will set, making caring for our clothes feel like a never-ending task. Get tough on stains: knowing you can care for investment pieces will give you the confidence to buy them in the first place – and take you further in your quest for a more conscious closet.

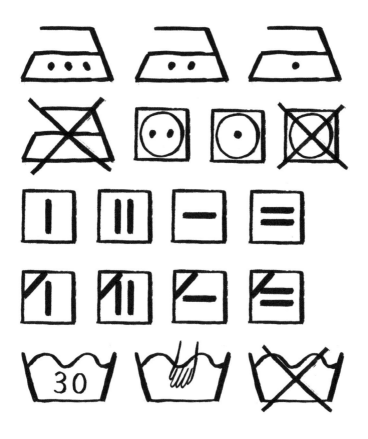

Check your clothing labels for instructions on how to wash,
dry and iron your clothes to keep them safe and spot-free.

Know what you're up against

When it comes to treating stains, it's all about speed, speed, speed. The quicker you remove stains, the better. Get familiar with common stains, so that you know the damage they cause and how to tackle them (grease, grass and grime each require different treatments, for example). The first action you take in stain removal will often determine if the stain will disappear completely or be fixed forever, so choose wisely.

As a rule, the most common stains, such as food or blood, should be rinsed immediately in cold water with a detergent, as hot water can fix the stain. Oily stains, however, such as hand cream and eggs, are best treated and then rinsed in hot water. Finally, liquids and food stains mustn't be rubbed – instead, dab, dab, dab (gently). And if you're thinking of chucking your stained garment straight into the machine, stop and look at how you can pre-treat the stain. Pre-treating beats the pants off just relying on your regular detergent.

Ditch chemical nasties

Most of us use chemically laden cleaning materials without a second thought, seduced by promises to 'bazooka' and 'blast' stains into the next century. Apply caution if using bleach (sodium hypochlorite): we tend to add bleach-based products to treat larger stains or whiten our whites, but bleach can be as aggressive on fibres as on stains, shortening the life of your textiles. So get tough on chemical use: don't just pick and choose, dump them altogether and opt for safer alternatives that won't contaminate waterways or take years to break down.

3

Naturally does it

Common stains and smells can be removed by using the simplest and cheapest natural ingredients, which are probably sitting in your kitchen already: bicarbonate of soda, white-wine vinegar, club soda and lemon juice all have great stain-removal properties. For delicate fabrics (or for those new to stain removal), try a spot test first to see how the treatment reacts before attacking the entire stain. If your cupboards are bare, look to the increasing number of brands that are working to bring natural alternatives to market, including Seventh Generation, Method and Ecover. If all else fails, if the stained item is white or a light-coloured fabric, try hanging it outside on a sunny day and let the sun do all the work.

4

Dye it

If you've tried and failed to eradicate a stain, why not try dyeing it? Home dyeing is quick and simple, and there are a kaleidoscope of colours to choose from. You can soak the garment to be dyed in a bucket, or in some cases add the dye to the washing-machine cycle. Just be sure that when choosing your dyes, you opt for environmentally friendly ones and avoid those with azo chemical compounds. Or go au naturel by using ingredients found in your kitchen or garden, such as strongly pigmented fruit and veg (blackberries, beetroot, butternut squash, and so on), flowers or tea bags. Whichever route you take, dyeing can bring your stained garment back into the fashion loop (see p. 95).

LAUREN SINGER

Lauren Singer's strong stance on landfill waste and her insistence on living a zero-waste life ensured her rise from Sustainability Manager at the NYC Department of Environmental Protection to pin-up girl for living consciously. She writes a popular blog, Trash Is For Tossers, and set up The Simply Co., which produces organic, vegan and non-toxic cleaning products.

'It's not just about paying attention to the sustainability factor of the clothes we buy, but also to what happens to them afterwards. If we are going to shop ethically, the clothes we buy deserve to be cleaned sustainably. As consumers, we have a right to products that are safe for our homes, our bodies and the environment. I hope to inspire people to ask why are there so many chemicals in everything, when did this become OK, and are they even necessary?'

Lauren's essentials for stain removal

Don't treat fire with fire

There are over 85,000 industrial chemicals out there, and the majority of them are not tested for safety before being released into the market. Plus, cleaning-product manufacturers are not legally required to list ingredients on their packaging. So don't reach for stain-removal products if you don't know what's in them, especially when there are so many toxic-free alternatives already in your kitchen cupboard. Try pre-treating the stain with some soap and water, or with a sustainable detergent.

Bicarb is your friend

Bicarbonate of soda (or baking soda, if you live Stateside) is another toxic-free stain-remover that you probably already have in your kitchen. It helps to draw stains out of the fabric and is particularly effective on wine, blood and odours.

Stock up on distilled white vinegar

Besides being an amazing all-purpose cleaner, this kitchen staple can be used to treat a multitude of stains, from grass to coffee to perfume. Depending on the size and type of stain, it can be added to a sinkful of water for pre-soaking clothes, or to the wash cycle, or mixed with cold water and applied directly to the stain.

Outdoor brand Patagonia operates the largest garment-repair facility in North America, and organizes workshops. Outside the US, customers can post their clothes for repair.

Zero-waste advocate Lauren Singer rose to fame after only producing one jar of trash in 12 months, and launching The Simply Co., which takes deadly chemicals out of detergents. (See her tips on p. 123).

Removing stains with bicarb

Lauren Singer

Create a stain-busting solution
by mixing 1 part bicarb with
3 parts water.

Using a brush (an old toothbrush
or nail brush will do), gently scrub
the stained area and leave for
20–30 minutes.

Place the garment into an
empty bucket and, from a
height, pour hot water over
it (but no hotter than your
fibres can handle).

Leave it to soak for
around an hour, or
30 minutes for delicates.

Wash the garment in
the machine as normal.

Recipe for a refresh spray

Redress

Take 1 tbsp baking
soda ...

... and 2 cups of
warm water (filtered
is better) ...

... and add 5–10 drops
of essential oil, shaking
it all up in a spray bottle.

Think before you wash

The way we do our laundry has shifted towards autopilot mode. Many of us habitually over-wash our clothes, even when they aren't dirty or smelly. The convenience of bunging our clothes into the machine has become so ingrained that we mistakenly believe that if our clothes don't smell of lavender fabric softener or some other manufactured fragrance, they must be absolutely filthy!

There are quick and easy ways to extend the time between machine washes, or prevent the need to wash altogether. The benefits are plentiful: the less you wash, the more time and money you save. Plus, you'll use less energy, water and detergents, all of which create negative environmental impacts. And by washing your clothes less, you will reduce general wear and tear – all of which will leave you and your clothes smelling of roses.

1

Wash less and live more!

Each time you subject a garment to the agitation of a wash cycle, colours fade and fibres weaken or disappear altogether, and its lifespan is reduced, one wash at a time. Scrutinize the item to see if it needs washing at all. If it does smell a bit, try refreshing it naturally first, then look for stains and spot-treat. If you still can't smell or see anything, why wash it?

To help you judge, consider your clothing's fibre types. Natural fabrics like cotton and silk are more absorbent and pull dirt and moisture deeper into the fibres, so they need more frequent washing. Polyester, however, is less absorbent and needs refreshing less frequently. Then consider how close the garment sits to your skin: the closer, the dirtier. Underwear and tops need washing more often than trousers, skirts, jackets and sweaters. But, as with everything in life, there are exceptions to the rules. Always launder off-season clothes before storage, even if they look clean, so that they don't attract insects while out of action (see pp. 166–71 for more on storage).

Air it, don't wash it

Air is free, so use it! Many garments with a slightly musty smell or marks from last night's revelries can be revived simply by airing them. Hang the offending garments anywhere that air can circulate, whether outside, on a balcony or next to an open window. This is an über-simple way of caring for your clothes and won't cost a cent or leave you with a hefty environmental footprint.

4

Brush it

If your clothes are generally clean but with a little surface fluff, dust or hair, use a reusable lint roller instead of going fibre-deep with a full wash. Or invest in a good clothing brush, which will do the job just as well on coats, jackets and trousers. A bit of effort will remove surface dirt and restore your garment to its former glory. This is an especially good tip for those with furry friends in the house.

3

Refresh it

If you're just dealing with the odd whiff but airing isn't doing the job, try neutralizing smells with a few spritzes of a fabric refresher. But think about which one you choose: many sprays are packed with chemicals such as sodium phosphate, which can irritate your skin – and you wouldn't want to inhale it. Instead, look for safer, toxic-free options like The Laundress, Mr Black and Washologi. Or take your quest for sustainability that little bit further by making your own (see p. 127 to learn how).

Spot-treat it

There is nothing more frustrating than getting a stain within a few hours of putting on a brand-new or freshly washed garment! But instead of washing the entire item, just treat the affected area. Your sweater or skirt will be back and ready for fashion-action quicker, without unnecessary water, energy and detergent usage (see p. 120 for more).

Shower with your delicates

If your handwashing always piles up, why not take your delicates with you into the shower for a quick handwash to save time, effort and water? Most shampoos, except those containing crème rinse, can deal with your lacy intimates just as well as your hair. Now you really can wash and go! But don't spoil all the potential water and energy savings; doing the laundry in the shower isn't an excuse to linger for longer.

ASH BLACK

Globetrotting entrepreneur Ash Black has been involved in many ventures, including the creation of the Green Hanger, a 100 per cent-recycled coat hanger. More recently, he has applied his energies to finding new solutions for washing his much-loved jeans. The result is Mr Black, a non-toxic, biodegradable range of products for refreshing, cleaning and protecting clothing, now available all over the world.

'I love and live in my jeans. Over the years, I've received many different, sometimes dubious, denim-cleaning tips, from not washing them at all to freezing them or walking into the ocean while wearing them! Along the way, I've tried and tested various ways to clean, most of which have kept my jeans out of the washing machine.'

Ash's essentials for washing denim

Wash jeans less
The less you wash your jeans, the better they adapt to your body, and the more you'll protect the fibres and colour from damage. How often you choose to machine-wash them will depend on your lifestyle, but I only machine-wash my jeans once a year.

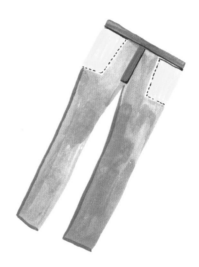

Turn your jeans inside out
If your jeans are slightly smelly, try turning them inside out and giving them a good old shake. Hanging them outside under the sun's UV light, ideally with a bit of breeze, will also help to freshen up the fibres.

Use refresher sprays
If stains and odours go deeper, there are plenty of great products out there. Spray them onto your denim to eliminate bacteria and neutralize odours, without the need for excessive water or energy use. They are quick and safe to use, so it's easy to keep your jeans clean without sticking them in the washing machine.

Ways for better washing

Washing clothes is unavoidable. But sloppy habits have caught up with us (just think of those shrunken woollens and whites that have gone pink) and contribute to excessive water and energy use. But there are ways to lighten your washing load that will save time, effort and money, and protect your clothes, allowing you to invest in your wardrobe and save the planet at the same time.

'I love my clothes much more than I love washing them! But I've learned the hard way that these things go hand in hand. Washing is payback time, and an opportunity to give clothes the TLC they deserve.'
Himarsha Venkatsamy, actress and model

1

Understand your machine

Unless you have the time and inclination to handwash your entire wardrobe, washing machines are an essential part of our lives. A good washing machine will both provide years of service and protect your clothes. It pays to invest in quality: some washing machines have a life expectancy of 20 years or more, whereas their budget counterparts may only last a fraction of that time, so choosing a good one will keep both your clothes and a succession of inferior machines out of landfill. Consider the value of the clothes that make up each of its loads: together, they could cost more than the machine itself, so look out for functions that can handle delicates such as wool, silk and cashmere. This will give you peace of mind and reduce your dry cleaning bills and environmental impact.

In general, newer machines tend to be more energy-efficient, but look for an A+ (or higher) energy rating. If you already own a machine, regardless of type, get to grips with its different cycle settings. Despite the multitude of programmes, most of us use the same one for everything, regardless of whether it is best suited to different loads or is the most environmentally sensitive. Finally, remember that your washing machine needs a little love and maintenance, so run a short, hot, detergent-free washing cycle every other month or so to give it a good clean and avoid build-up of bacteria and mould. Add a cup of lemon juice to help keep rust spots at bay.

2

To handwash or not?

Wise up to what requires hand- or machine-washing to avoid seeing your silks reduced to rags and your knits to miniature versions of their former selves. Silk, satin and lace are generally best handwashed whenever possible, as some washing machines, particularly older or poorer quality ones, can damage delicate fabrics through the heavy pounding they receive during the spin cycle. And to add to the confusion, many clothes that say 'dry clean only' may be handwashed. If you have a top-quality washing machine with a handwash cycle, you may be able to trust it to do the job for you (see also p. 143).

3

Divide and conquer

When sorting your laundry, be sure to separate whites, darks and colours. Bright-coloured clothes and new, dark-coloured ones love to share their pigments with others, so wash like with like. And if you have enough in the laundry basket to warrant it, divide clothes further into different fabric types and use the appropriate washing programme. There's no point in putting a single polyester or cotton item through the wash on its own, however, so in that case mix fibres up to avoid wasting water. Just thinking about all of those pink 'whites' will give you the motivation you need to get sorting!

Prevention is better than cure

Protecting your clothes, especially delicates, with simple tricks before they are sent whirling through the machine will pay dividends. Underwired bras, tights, sequinned items and other delicates are best slipped into a separate laundry bag, which will both reduce the mechanical whiplash endured during a machine cycle and protect garments from catching on zips and buttons. Plus, placing your tights into a laundry bag will avoid the tangled knot of tights and trousers! Denim and embellished clothes are best turned inside out when washing to reduce the risk of damage. And finally, it's best to button and zip up your clothes before washing to help protect their shape.

Think before you load

Getting load sizes right is key to getting the best from your washing machine. Many machines use the same amount of water and energy for all of their cycles, regardless of how much or less you fill them, making small loads very wasteful. As a general rule, most machines must run at full to derive their maximum energy- and water-efficiency. Some high-tech machines, however, can auto-adjust their water and energy usage according to different load sizes. Study the instructions to find out the ideal capacity for your machine, and avoid over- or under-loading.

Get tough on softeners

We add fabric softeners to the wash to get our clothes smelling fresher and feeling softer, and to reduce static cling. But just like detergents, apart from the few products that contain natural alternatives, fabric softeners are made from a cocktail of toxic chemicals. Try to eliminate softeners altogether or, if you're addicted to a softer touch, use environmentally friendly alternatives. You can add a scoop of bicarb or white wine vinegar to your washing machine to soften your clothes (don't worry, you won't smell like a chippie), or line dry them to remove static cling. Or, to get the scent of softeners without the toxic chemicals, add a few drops of essential oils stirred into a little water to the softener drawer of your machine.

Use the correct amount

How you measure your detergent matters. In fact, with the scary array of detergents out there that contain nasty ingredients like phenols, optical brighteners and bleaches, it really matters. Choose environmentally friendly detergents, such as Ecover, The Simply Co. or Laundress (see Resources), which aren't packed with toxic chemicals. And always use the recommended amount: any more won't get your clothes any cleaner and just clogs up your washing machine's internal plumbing. Alternatively, you could ditch the detergent altogether and try soap nuts, the fruit of a tree found in the Himalayas, which you add to your wash in a small bag. They last around four to five washes before needing to be replaced, and are a great option for those with allergies or sensitive skin.

Temperature matters

Many of us automatically wash at 40° C (104° F), or higher. This is effectively flushing our cash down the drain as we waste money on heating the water, not to mention the higher risk of damaging our clothes. Instead, lower the temperature to 30° C (86° F), or even cooler for delicate fibres such as cashmere or silk. Most modern machines and detergents can clean efficiently at this temperature, especially if you pre-treat any tougher stains. For hygienically challenged items (underwear, bedlinen or clothes that went through a gruelling gym session or a serious case of gastroenteritis), you might want to wash at a higher temperature (40–60° C, or 104–140° F).

Time it right

Life is busy! With all the living to do, it's easy to forget to take freshly washed and wet clothes out of the machine. But it's always best to remove your clothes promptly once the cycle has completed to protect both them and the machine. Leaving wet clothes in the drum even for a few hours allows time for creases and odours to set in. Plus, as your wet clothes wallow in the machine they can pick up rust stains.

EVA KRUSE

As CEO of the Danish Fashion Institute, Eva Kruse promotes sustainable and socially responsible fashion on platforms such as the Copenhagen Fashion Summit, launched during the 2009 UN Climate Change Conference. She has been a TV presenter in Denmark and editor-in-chief of *Eurowoman* magazine, and in 2013 gave a TEDx talk, 'Changing the World Through Fashion'. She also serves on the board of the Nordic Fashion Association.

'Consumers have the power to change the industry and the environment. Even the little things we do count. Although small changes may seem insignificant, everything we do, say and buy has an effect. Simple actions, like line drying your laundry and washing your clothes less frequently and at lower temperatures, allow us to be agents of change.'

Eva's essentials for better washing habits

Change your mindset
We spend a lot of our time thinking about what clothes to buy, but not enough on how to care for them once we do buy them. By dedicating more thought to the care of our clothes, they will reward us by staying in top condition and in our closets for longer.

Measure carefully
Use a toxic-free washing detergent to protect your clothes and the environment. And use the correct amount! In our effort to get our clothes clean we tend to use too much detergent. Instead, follow the manufacturer's guidelines so that you are not throwing both money and valuable resources down the drain.

Reduce the temperature
Washing your clothes at a lower temperature reduces carbon-dioxide emissions and your electricity bill, while still getting the stains out. Laundry is one of the most energy-consuming processes in our households, so washing at 30° C (86° F) will make a real difference. If every household in Europe reduced their washing temperature from 60° or 40° C (140° or 104° F), we could save 12 million tonnes of carbon dioxide a year, the same amount of emissions as three million cars.

Sustainable fashion advocate Eva Kruse takes as firm a stance on treating stains as she does creating her red-carpet looks. (See her tips on p. 141).

'Ninety per cent of the items in our wardrobes are washable, even if the label says dry clean only. We have found that with the right products it is easy to care for clothes at home and reduce the need for dry cleaning.' – Gwen Whiting and Lindsey J. Boyd, The Laundress

Dry it better

Drying clothes is a necessity. But too often in our fast-paced lives we flip wet clothes from washing machine to tumble dryer automatically, without a thought for more energy-efficient drying options. While tumble dryers do indeed dry your clothes quickly, they are also greedy kilowatt consumers, so what they gain in speed, you lose in money spent on paying your electricity bills. And then there's the increased wear and tear on your clothes, as fibres are caught in the filter. Opt instead for alternative drying methods that forgo the tumble dryer and reduce your electricity bill and your carbon footprint.

1

Dry with care

The drying process can be dangerous for delicate garments, so you need to know the drying likes and dislikes of different clothing types in order to protect them. Some clothes need extra care during drying to avoid changes to their shape or size. Heat-sensitive fibres such as wool and cashmere will shrink in a heated tumble dryer, leaving you with miniature versions of your clothes. Knitwear can easily lose its shape if hung out wet, so lay it out flat to prevent stretching.

2

Hang it out to dry

Line drying is an old favourite because it works. It saves money that would otherwise be spent on unnecessary electricity and reduces carbon-dioxide emissions, and it extends the life of your clothes by not subjecting them to the wear and tear inflicted during tumble drying. Line drying your whites in the sun goes one step further, because UV light is a good sterilizing agent. But be careful when it comes to darks: to avoid fading, don't hang dark clothes in bright sunlight and be sure to turn them inside out, which also speeds up the drying process if they have bulky pockets. Finally, avoid creating marks on your clothes by clipping pegs onto less visible areas, and eliminate rusty pegs altogether.

3

Bring the 'line' indoors

Don't be put off line drying if you lack outside space or if the weather isn't on your side. A compact, foldaway clothes rack is great for indoor use, particularly in your home's warmest spot, whether the bedroom, living room, or even the bathroom. Hang wrinkle-prone garments like silk and linen on hangers and hook them onto the rack. You can also use your home's heat source – radiators, airing cupboards – to dry your clothes. This is great for winter, when line drying outside isn't an option and you'll probably have the heat on inside anyway. While these drying options take a bit longer, it's worth the wait as you reduce your energy bills and increase the shininess of your environmental halo.

4

Tumble dry efficiently

If you must use a tumble dryer, then it's worth investing in a high-quality, energy-efficient model, which will give you the best results with the smallest impact. Regardless of the type of dryer you have, remember to remove lint from the filter after every use, as this increases your machine's efficiency and shortens drying time, saving you time and money.

SUMMER RAYNE OAKES

Fashion and beauty expert Summer Rayne Oakes counts model, author, TV presenter, designer, producer and entrepreneur among her many other hats, and has been named everything from 'Top Environmental Activist' to one of the 'Top 20 Trendsetters under 40' and '10 Best Green Entrepreneurs'. When not writing for *The New York Times* or working on photoshoots for *Vogue*, she produces her own podcast in her quest to make sustainability a natural part of our lives.

'I've been line drying my clothes for as long as I can remember, so it's part of my clothing-care routine wherever I am in the world. It is a huge energy-saver and a no-brainer, environmentally and financially. It also gets me outside, even if it's just a rooftop or balcony.'

Summer Rayne's essentials for line drying

Size isn't everything!

I've been drying my clothes without the aid of a tumble dryer in my New York apartment for years now, so a lack of space is no excuse. There seem to be as many different types of drying racks, from compact to expandable, as clothes in your closet. If your room won't fit a rack, put up a line in your living room or hang clothes out to dry from a window.

Keep it fresh

Freshly washed clothes soak up powerful smells as they dry (think curry cooking in the kitchen and cars revving on the roads), so be sure to position them well away from such odours.

Time your drying right

If you have guests and you don't want them more interested in your laundry than in your cooking, hang your clothes out the night before so that they're dry when you come home from work. Speed the drying process by positioning the rack to get some sunlight, and don't overlap damp clothes on the rail or line.

Summer Rayne Oakes manages her carefully curated closet the old-fashioned way: by line-drying her clothes, and protecting them in the process. (See her tips on p. 149).

Follow Summer Rayne's example and choose the environmentally friendly option by line-drying your clothes on a line or inside on a drying rack.

De-crease with ease

The need to eradicate creases and wrinkles –
on your clothes, at least – is here to stay. Let's face
it, crumpled chic has yet to catch on, which means
the energy- and time-guzzling iron is, too. And the
potential hazards don't end there: a careless slip of
the hand can brand clothes with that familiar iron-
shaped burn mark and rusty splatters. But there are
de-creasing tricks and tips that can compete with the
iron's performance, with some even doing away with
the need to iron at all.

1

Be selective
It may sound obvious, but only iron what you absolutely need to. We often reach automatically for the iron as part of our clothing-care routine, but many fabrics, such as polyester, wool, Tencel and the new generation of wrinkle-free fabrics, don't need it.

2

Hang it up
It's best to hang your clothes up while they are still wet, so that you put gravity to work on creases right away. Hang immediately after washing: for wrinkle-prone fabrics like linen, try cancelling the final spin cycle or using a less intensive spin, so that the contents emerge wetter than usual from the washing machine. But take note: this rule does not apply to wool and cashmere, which instead must be laid out flat to dry.

Starch naturally

For certain items, such as shirts, you might want to have crisper collars and cuffs. To do so, you don't need to buy a conventional spray starch, which will only add to the total you pay at the till and are often full of toxic chemicals. Instead, do as Bea Johnson (author of the Zero Waste Home blog) does and make your own starch solution for next to nothing: dissolve 1 tbsp of cornstarch (go organic here, if possible) in a pint of water, then pour the mixture into a spray bottle ready to spritz onto your shirts. It worked for your grandparents, and it will work for you, too!

Steam it

You can even do the 'ironing' while singing in the shower! Some lighter fabrics, like cotton, polyester and silk, can be rid of creases by simply putting them on a hanger in the bathroom and letting the steam do all the work for you. This is a particularly good trick when travelling, when clothes often emerge after a flight or car journey as crumpled as their owners. Clever, simple and effective.

Invest in a good iron

If you still feel the need to reach for the iron on a regular basis, it's worth investing in a good, energy-efficient model. As well as keeping your energy consumption down, it will also protect your clothes, since older and poorer quality irons have a tendency to spit water, adding unwanted rusty stains.

Don't iron and run

If you've just ironed your clothes, wait until the garment has completely cooled down – five minutes should do it – before putting it on and rushing off. If you put on a still-hot garment, you'll just create more wrinkles.

Maintenance and repair

Our clothes will inevitably suffer wear and tear as they travel with us through our lives, but all too often we fail to look after them properly. This is partly because buying new clothes has never been cheaper or easier, but also because we have lost the skills needed to repair them. Instead of reaching for a needle and thread, it's more convenient to reach for our wallets. But many clothes are now so inferiorly produced that they need all the TLC they can get.

You'll need to recalibrate your maintenance-and-repair mindset if you want a stylish conscious closet. By now hopefully you're inspired to buy less and buy better, and will be wanting to compile a higher-quality wardrobe that will need to be cared for. Doing so properly enables you to avoid many of the routine signs of wear and tear, leaving you with less clothing waste and more fashion return on your investment.

Give your closet its own tool kit

It's essential to have some basic tools to hand to ensure that mending and maintaining your conscious closet is satisfying, rather than frustrating. Your tool kit should contain, at the minimum, some needles, thread in a few basic colours, a sharp pair of scissors, spare buttons and some polish and brushes for your shoes, bags and belts. Also good to have on hand are a snag-repair tool (for pulling loose threads through to the reverse side of fabrics) and iron-on interfacing for strengthening fabric.

Learn the basics of mending

Some issues that regularly occur are loose or missing buttons, thinning or fraying fabrics, and detached or dragging hems. For most repairs, get started by turning your garment inside out and thread your needle. You can double the thread to stop it slipping out of the needle and to add strength to your stitches – just don't forget to tie a knot at the end! Now get sewing. You will need to get the hang of a few basic stitches – running, blind, whip (head to YouTube for online tutorials) – as these will come in handy for many different repairs. When finishing off a section, tie off the thread securely by bringing your needle through to the reverse of the fabric and sliding it underneath a few stitches. Before pulling the thread tight, slip the needle back though the loop, tug and repeat to ensure the stitches don't unravel along with your good work.

3

Let the iron be your needle

For those who are all thumbs when it comes to needlework, try iron-on interfacing to repair and reinforce your clothes. This nifty material is ironed onto the fabric's reverse side to reinforce weaker areas before fully fledged holes appear. Try double-sided adhesive webbing for speedy hemming. When ironing on either of these materials, use a layer of scrap fabric or a tea towel between them and the iron to avoid damage to the hot plate caused by any leaking glue. Finally, secure the interface in place with a few small stitches to help it last longer.

Get creative on damage!

For severely damaged areas that need more than a few stitches to return garments to working order, give your clothes a new personality altogether by trying out a visible repair. You could add beautiful detailing, such as stitching in a contrasting colour or patches and trims to create an interesting feature. These are great ways of turning a tricky repair job into a purposeful change.

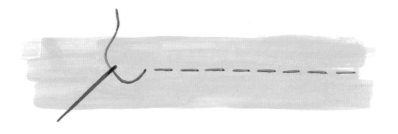

Save your hemlines

A hanging hemline is not a hanging offence! Yet many people chuck their clothes away simply because of a loose hemline. Just get a needle, some thread (as close to the garment's colour as possible), some pins and an iron. Before stitching, iron the hem back into position to ensure it hangs straight. Then use a simple blind stitch to hide larger stitches out of sight, leaving visible only small ones at the front. If you're feeling unsure, check out online hemming tutorials. Remember, most of the time you'll only be hemming the damaged part of the hem – if you catch it early, that is. But always start your repair further back from where the hem has come loose, and secure any old threads. If using interface, keep an eye on it once you've done your repair, as it will need replacing more often.

Look for damaged linings

Look out for wear to the inside of a garment, as well. Linings, especially on coats and jackets, can become ripped or loose, particularly under the armpits. But these rips are easily mended by simple hand-sewing. First, give the area to be worked on a quick press with the iron, and pin the rip or split seam back together. Then get to work with a catch stitch: take a little fabric from each side of the rip and zigzag from one end to the other until the tear is closed. The good news is that because the rips, and therefore your stitches, are on the inside, no one will see if your work is a bit messy.

Repair your knits ...

Catching damage to knitwear early is important: when left to its own devices a small snag can quickly turn into a big hole. Often the first sign of trouble is a stray thread that pops out of your jumper. Act fast! Simply pull the thread through to the inside, using a snag-repair tool or any other gently pointed implement (such as a knitting needle or skewer). Then anchor the wayward thread by tying it off.

Next up, tacking holes. To do this, you'll need to turn your hand to darning, which is different from conventional stitching, and needs patience and confidence. First, match your wool to the garment. The idea is not to close up a hole by pulling in the edges, but to create a mesh of threads that fill up the hole. As with most repairs, work on the reverse side, and use a rounded object (a cup or tennis ball) underneath to support the garment as you're working.

Then get darning! This involves creating lots of stitches using a simple running stitch: think of a worm wriggling back and forth over the space to create parallel lines. Then 'weave' perpendicular stitches into your mesh. While it may sound old-fashioned, darning is a clever way to close a hole with the least visibility.

... and look after your shoes

Shoes can get heavily worn, especially around the heels and tips. Prevention, via regular cleaning, waxing and good storage, is better than cure, so stock up on protective canvas bags, shoe trees, polish and a good set of cleaning brushes. You can also make your own natural alternatives at home: try rubbing olive oil into the leather once a week, adding beeswax to the mix for extra protection. Some even swear by rubbing the inside of a banana peel on leather to provide a natural shine. To further extend the life of your shoes, take them to a cobbler, who can replace worn-down heels and tips. As with all maintenance, it's important to check your shoes regularly so that you catch any signs of damage before it's too late.

9

Protect your outer layers

More durable items such as raincoats and leather bags require extra TLC in the shape of a regular wax or polish to keep them in tip-top condition. Think of waxing and polishing as the equivalent to applying an anti-aging cream. But just as with skincare, many of the polishes on the market today contain toxic chemicals that aren't good for people or the planet. Read the fine print and when in doubt, go for products with natural ingredients, such as beeswax. Wipe first with a damp cloth to remove any residue before applying wax.

10

Take it in for service

If the necessary repair feels too big to do on your own, get help. You could bring your damaged clothes to a sewing café, where you'll get both a helping hand and a cup of tea. If you'd rather get a professional to take on the job, take your damaged clothes to a tailor. Or you could even take them back to the manufacturer: some brands (such as Nudie Jeans and Patagonia) offer mending as part of their customer service or even include repairs for the life of the item in the price tag. So check your favourite brands to see if they offer repair services. If they don't, ask why not.

FIONA KOTUR

Designer Fiona Kotur launched her accessories company Kotur in 2005, now stocked in over 30 countries worldwide. She has worked with Ralph Lauren, Gap and Tory Burch, and her designs are regularly worn by Hollywood A-listers. Fiona has been featured in *Vanity Fair*'s International Best-dressed List and was named a 'Woman of Hope' by Hong Kong *Tatler* for her philanthropic efforts.

'I take pride in caring for things and believe that, like relationships, one's clothes need nurturing. I rarely discard anything, and when I do buy something new, my intention is that it lasts, whether it is an investment piece or a high-street brand, both of which feature in my wardrobe. With each item carefully chosen and cared for, my ownership can last for many years (I still have my mother's Gucci handbags from the 1960s!)'

Fiona's essentials for a maintenance mindset

Keep them covered

I'm fastidious about keeping my shoes and bags well maintained, and clean and polish them regularly, which allows me to inspect them for damage. I also store them in shoe boxes and garment bags to protect them further.

A cobbler you trust

It's important to repair shoes if they are damaged, and to attend to worn-down heels or loose straps and buckles as quickly as possible. It's certainly worth paying a professional to help with repairs as the transformations they can produce are quite amazing.

From the inside out

Even when you're not wearing them, you need to be careful with your accessories. I stuff acid-free paper inside bags and shoes to preserve their shape, and always use shoe trees when I travel to protect shoes from damage during transit.

Regular maintenance is key to helping Fiona Kotur keep her wardrobe of designer and high-street pieces pristine, and she uses shoe trees and garment bags to help them last for years.

Serial entrepreneur and denim aficionado Ash Black is the brains behind Mr Black, a range of garment-care products that help to protect clothes and extend the time between washing cycles.

Practise better storage

Clothes need to be stored properly, both in the wardrobe for everyday use and packed away when out of season. Cramming them into closets and squashing them into suitcases will cause damage, and can lead to the appearance of unwelcome guests in the form of moths. Inadequate storage makes getting dressed harder, because you have to battle just to find your clothes, let alone decide what to wear.

Instead, storing your clothes away systematically will pay dividends. By carefully folding, packing and hanging garments, you will protect their shape and keep mould and critters away. You will also be able to hang on to your clothing's financial value, and keep them in the fashion loop and out of landfill for longer.

1

Clothes need space, too

Overstuffed wardrobes can damage your clothes by leaving them misshapen, crushed, wrinkled, even mouldy. To prevent this, always hang, fold, pack and store your clothes loosely to allow air to circulate. If you have enough space, store your off-season and special-occasion clothes in a separate area of the house, so that they – and you, on a rushed morning – have more space to breathe.

2

Fold or hang?

It's important to know which clothes to fold and which to hang. Some garments, like knitwear, wool or heavier items with thin straps, get damaged when hung in the wardrobe simply through their own weight, as gravity causes the fabric to stretch around the neck and shoulder area. Instead, fold and stack knitwear, placing the heaviest items at the bottom and the lightest at the top.

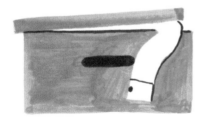

3

Hang it right

Invest in good quality, well-shaped hangers to help your clothes maintain their correct shape. Thin wire hangers become bent, and can stretch some fabrics by not providing enough support. Padded or wooden hangers will give your garments the support they need, with padded hangers best for fragile garments, such as chiffon tops and silk dresses, and sturdy wooden hangers with broad sides especially good for heavier items like coats. Hangers with clips are useful for bottoms, but go for those with an added layer of protective sponge-like material on the grip so that they don't leave marks.

4

Protect your delicates

Lace and silk garments, with or without added embellishments or trimmings, need protection from clothes made from rougher fabrics – and from the rough edges of the wardrobe itself. Divide your closet space into sections, or protect delicates by stashing them away in garment bags.

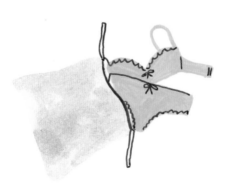

Keep in shape

Our accessories often don't receive the extra TLC they need to enjoy as long a life as possible. To keep your shoes in mint condition, stuff them with newspaper and store them upright. Then give your bags, whether or not they are from a designer or the high street, the same love and attention. Fill them with rolled-up old T-shirts or scrunched newspaper to protect their shape, and then wrap them in a cloth bag to help ward off scratches.

Use the right protection

Clothes need protection, too. But remember that even in storage, fibres need to breathe. Avoid plastic covers and bags, which prevent air circulation and trap in moisture, creating the perfect breeding ground for mould and mildew, and even changes in colour. Instead, store clothes in breathable cotton garment bags. If you're low on space, you could try vacuum bags, which are available in most hardware stores. But while this method shrinks bags down to size, the bags are usually made of plastic and don't allow clothes to breathe, so check on them periodically for signs of damage.

7

Clean, then store

When storing out-of-season clothes, be sure to wash them first, even if they don't appear or smell as if they need it. If left uncleaned, the residual sweat, food and dirt can attract unwelcome visitors in the form of insects. Avoid over-the-counter mothballs, as they have an unpleasant odour and can contain naphthalene, a flammable and toxic chemical. Instead, try cedar balls or lavender sachets to keep your items smelling sweet and safe from pests.

Go steady with storage

Keeping the condition your clothes are stored in as stable as possible is important. So don't hang them or place storage boxes near windows, because persistent exposure to sunlight can fade and weaken fibres. If you're using a basement, attic or outdoor storage unit, watch out for changes in temperature, which can likewise damage clothes. Humidity can also wreak havoc, as moisture is absorbed into the fibres, leading to the appearance of mould and mildew. To combat this, try adding a pouch of charcoal in the storage area to absorb moisture.

Dispose

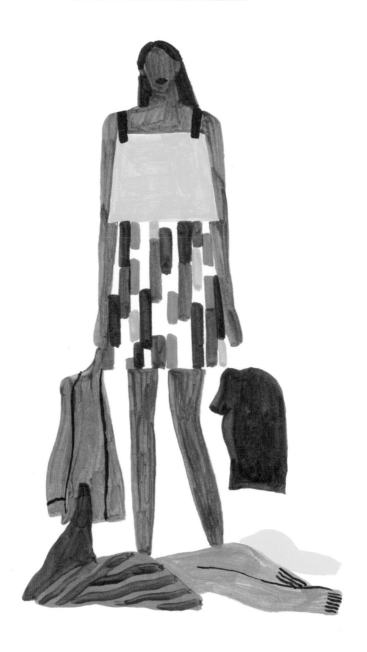

The reality

Getting rid of unwanted clothes is a bit like trying to cure a giant hangover caused by fashion consumption. After the high of each fashion 'fix', the morning after sees discarded clothes being sent packing to landfills or incinerators, or (apart from a small percentage) flooding into developing countries via the charity shop. As we consume more, so too do we waste more, as seemingly 'old' clothes make way for new – we buy a shocking 400 per cent more clothes than we did two decades ago.[24] In the US alone, landfills have seen a 38 per cent increase in textile waste over an 11-year period; during the same period, overall waste to landfill decreased by 1 per cent.[25]

Dumping clothes into landfill causes a number of problems, as many clothes now contain non-biodegradable synthetic fibres, such as polyester and nylon. Just like plastic bottles, these clothes hang around for decades and, in some cases, centuries. In addition, our clothing cast-offs, along with the rest of the rubbish piling up in landfills, emit polluting gases that contribute to climate change. And depending on where you live, your old clothes could be burned in incinerators along with the household rubbish – an incredibly wasteful process.

Each time we burn our clothes or take them to landfill, we also throw away the oil, water, chemicals, pesticides, electricity and labour that went into making them. This same wasteful concept applies when we hoard clothes, rather than wear them, as we are essentially locking all of these resources into a state of disuse. And for what?

Even if we don't destroy unwanted clothes and donate them instead, our over-consumption of cheap, poorly produced goods means that this is the quality of clothing being routinely sent to developing countries. Although this practice promotes reuse before recycling, and is in theory better for the environment than disposal, the reality is that such largesse can stifle local textile and garment industries, rather than being the generous gesture intended. These wasteful scenarios – sending goods to landfills, burning and dumping, often on other nations' doorsteps – are alarming and unsustainable, given that the earth's natural resources are becoming ever scarcer. Our shop-til-you-drop mentality is perpetuating a rapacious cycle of new clothing production, which is not only killing the planet, but people too.

'More and more of us treat clothes like disposable items, but they really aren't. If we choose our clothes with care, we can swap, resell and donate them onwards. Quality clothes have so much more life and fun left in them!'
Marieke Eyskoot,
sustainable fashion and lifestyle expert

Here's what you need to know...

We throw too much away

Our alarming habit of throwing clothes away before their time means that European consumers discard 5.8 million tonnes of textiles per year.[26] In China, the total production of pre- and post-consumer textile waste is estimated at around 26 million tonnes per year.[27]

We don't recycle enough

Around 95 per cent of consumers' textile waste can be reused or recycled.[29] In terms of environmental benefits, recycling textiles is second only to recycling aluminium, because the embedded energy in them is so valuable.[30] This constitutes a missed opportunity for textiles to be reused, repaired or remade into 'new' products.

Waste ends up in the wrong hands

We are not fully considering the final destination of our discarded clothes. Only 25 per cent of the textiles that EU consumers dispose of each year are recycled by charities and industrial enterprises. The remaining 4.3 million tonnes go to landfill or are burnt in incinerators.[28]

We waste resources

When we throw clothes away, we also chuck out all of the natural and human resources invested in the fabric of our clothes. For example, by collecting 1 kg (2.2 lbs) of used clothing, we could reduce 3.6 kg (8 lbs) of CO_2 emissions, 6,000 litres (1,320 gallons) of water, 0.3 kg (10.5 oz.) of fertilizers and 0.2 kg (7 oz.) of pesticides, which would otherwise be created by the production of new garments.[31]

We waste money

These wasted resources could be put back into the economy and into our pockets. In the UK, an estimated £140 million ($184 million) worth of used clothing goes to landfill every year, and China's annual textile waste is estimated to be worth RMB 66 billion (£7 billion, or $9.2 million).[32]

We waste our wardrobes

All those unworn clothes huddled at the back of our wardrobes represent lost value. Around 30 per cent of the clothes in a typical British household haven't been worn for at least a year, representing over £1,000 ($1,300) of wasted clothing value – or a whopping £30 billion ($39.4 billion) across the UK.[35]

We pollute the environment

In addition to clogging up landfills, textile waste also contributes to environmental pollution. Certain synthetic fibres, like polyester and nylon, take a very long time to decompose (or never do), while natural fibres such as cotton and wool do decompose but produce methane, a major contributor to climate change.[33] Just imagine: it can take 30 to 40 years for nylon fabric to decompose and six months for a cotton T-shirt.[34]

Things you can do

While this sorry glimpse into our global clothing waste might seem too large to tackle alone, we do have power. Much of the textile waste created could be avoided through simple repairs, better consumer care and increased efforts to collect and reuse secondhand clothing and footwear. The world is waking up to how valuable and useful clothing 'waste' is.

More charities, communities and companies are collecting unwanted clothing, because reusing clothes has many benefits, particularly when competition for natural resources is high. Plus, there are many more clever advances today in clothing and textile recycling that can transform unwanted clothes into 'new' materials, from coats to carpets. We can all play our part in reducing clothing waste. Power to the people!

This is where you – the conscious consumer – come in. There are many creative ways to implement the 'reduce, reuse and recycle' mantra in your closet. Free up your unwanted and unworn clothes to support good causes and be part of what you really believe in! The following disposal options should inspire you to swap, gift, sell, donate and rethink your textile waste, while also benefiting your conscience, cash flow, closet and, of course, our shared environment.

'I changed my approach to the disposal of unwanted clothes radically after witnessing firsthand the true cost of what both the planet and people invest into fashion. Unconsidered disposal of clothes is a disrespectful way to treat the lives who made them.'

Andrew Morgan, filmmaker

The time it takes for our clothes to decompose

Cotton 1–5 months

Nylon 30–40 years

Leather 30–40 years

Polyester 200+ years

Wool 1–5 years

Swap it

Fashion tastes may change, but some things stay the same. Many of us have quality clothes that we hang onto long after we've stopped wearing them. As a result, our wardrobes contain barely worn clothes that could become fashion-active in someone else's hands. So why not try swapping? It clears your closet, at least temporarily, of unwanted clothes, while also giving you the buzz of acquiring 'new' on your journey towards compiling a low-impact, high-appeal closet. And all of this comes for free! Plus swapping parties are inherently sociable. It's no wonder converts say, 'swapping is better than shopping'.

Get your closet ready

First, search your wardrobe for clothes that are ready to be transformed into swapping currency. Good candidates are quality clothes that are free from stains and damage, because you'll want to be proud, not embarrassed, to hand them over to your friends, family and fellow swappers. Other people's styles vary hugely, so just because something has slipped in your fashion esteem doesn't mean it won't be treasured by someone else. If finding swap-worthy clothes is a challenge, start the process by doing a closet edit (see pp. 72–7).

Get on the guest list

Look out for swapping events in your local area – more and more of them are cropping up around the world, hosted by individuals or organizations. There are also online swapping websites, such as Swapdom and Vinted, so you can swap with people of all styles, shapes and sizes across the globe. Naturally, to keep your swapping low-carbon, go local to reduce your shipping impacts.

Organize your own swap

If you want to get a bit more hands-on, try organizing a swap of your own. Keep it small by inviting a couple of friends over for coffee, or take it up a notch and invite your extended group of friends and family. Or you could really think big, and involve your community by holding a swap at a school, café or village hall. But regardless of scale, cast your net wide when compiling your guest list. Guests will arrive in varying sizes, silhouettes and styles, so ensure they have plenty of choice and are able to leave with garments that fit.

Planning is key: give your guests time to sort and prepare their loot beforehand and give clear guidance on your credit system. Will you need to charge an entry fee to cover costs? Or you could suggest donations to a favourite charity instead. Finally, you'll enjoy the swap more if clothes are neatly presented, with plenty of mirrors, so the thrill of the chase isn't tempered by chaos. Setting the scene allows you to catch up with friends, while having fun trying out new styles and sharing tips.

Understand the system

Whether attending a swap or organizing your own, know how the credit system works so that you can best assess your swapping stock. It pays off if there is a fair system in place. The simplest is one-for-one, where for every one item brought into the swap you get one credit, which allows you to take one item out.

Or you might employ a system that rewards quality by grading items into 'value' categories, giving swappers the corresponding amount of swapping credits. For example, luxury clothes get 15 credits, mid-range garments 10 credits and high-street wares 5 credits. Whichever system you choose, the ultimate aim is to provide an enjoyable experience so that swappers come away with 'new' clothes and smiles on their faces, pledging never to return to the shops.

Consider the leftovers

Once the swap is over, there is bound to be a pile of unswapped clothes left behind that still have plenty of fashion life in them. Don't let them go to waste! Support the organizers by offering ideas for the post-swap clear up, ensuring that the leftover clothes continue supporting good causes (see pp. 196–203).

Resell it

Many of us are sitting on, but not wearing, a goldmine of great clothes, justifying this with excuses like 'it doesn't fit' or 'I don't like it anymore'. We might be holding onto them because of their great quality, and possibly regret how much we spent on them. But learn to let go! It makes sense, financially and environmentally, to say goodbye to pieces that, for whatever reason, you no longer treasure.

You may be pleasantly surprised at the value of what's lying dormant in your closet, and by how much others are willing to spend on it. Recapitalize some of the cash you invested in your closet, while releasing clothes back into the fashion loop for someone else to benefit from.

'Every year, I hold a Shop-in-my-Closet Love Fest, and sell clothes to friends who will enjoy wearing them in the spirit of recycling and renewal. All the money goes to charity: it may be a small gesture, but it's hugely rewarding.'
Bandana Tewari, Fashion Features Director, *Vogue India*

Be ruthless, but realistic

The first step in selling is deciding what you want to sell and whether it's worth the effort. Don't keep clothes if you don't wear them, but be realistic about your market: do you really think others will buy it? Remember, what you consider outdated might just be what someone else is looking for. When it comes to selling, evaluate the brand. It's no surprise that well-known designer names sell better than high-street brands. Niche, lesser-known brands may be trickier to sell because customers may not have heard of them. When thinking about specific items to sell, popular items in the resale market are quality jeans, vintage T-shirts and leather bags.

Present in mint condition

Yes, your purchaser may be buying a used item, but she'll get more pleasure from it, and pay more for it, if she feels she is buying 'new'. The basic rules to ensure happy and returning customers are to sell secondhand items clean, complete and in good condition. They want your vintage rock T-shirt, but not the accompanying signs of the good time you had partying in it! Check your wares for smells, stains, rips and loose buttons, and deal with these before offering them up for sale (see chapter 3 for more on clothing care). Finally, presentation is key. It's a bonus if you've got the original packaging, particularly for branded and luxury items, as this upgrades the secondhand shopping experience.

3

Get price savvy

Setting your price calls for some research. What you sell an item for and how much you pocket depend on the quality of the goods and the type of retail platform you use, whether a physical shop or an online auction site. Know what your clothes are worth by checking out similar items. You'll also need to get savvy on the trading system you use. Some resale platforms give you cash, while others give you store credit. If you like the action of online auction sites, then go for it! Set your opening bid low to attract interest. Once the bidding kicks off, you may be surprised at what others are willing to pay.

4

Sell your seconds online

If you have the time and great quality clothes to sell, then online platforms will instantly connect them with a larger customer base. There are many online platforms to choose from, including thredUP and BuyMyWardrobe, with most taking a commission. How you list your wares online is crucial to optimizing searchability and bringing the buyers to you. Use keywords and detailed titles to describe your garment, and brand name-dropping is must. Be clear about sizing and use well-lit images, so that buyers get a clear view of what's on offer.

5

6

Match with the seasons

If you want to sell quickly and at a good price, timing is important. Sell your seconds during their correct season, when market demand is highest. Your bikini may be difficult to shift in the winter, as will your wool coat in summer. If you want to sell like a professional, you may need to put your secondhand items on ice for a while (see pp. 166–71 for more on storage), until the correct season comes round again.

Set up shop

If you have a larger stash of clothes to sell and you want to shift them quickly, why not set up shop? The best places to shift stock are at locations with high foot traffic, such as car-boot sales, flea markets or stalls within pre-existing markets. Set up alone or join forces – and add to the fun – with a friend. Before setting up shop, price your clothes. Be prepared for bargaining, which is all part of the fun of market selling! Alternatively, you could organize a garage sale. For this, you'll need to do some local marketing – think signs, posters, flyers – to help customers come to you.

7

Let others do the selling

If you're short on time and have high-quality garments to sell, the quickest and easiest option is to get someone else to do the legwork for you. Consignment stores, which are secondhand boutiques run by a middleman who does the selling, can either have a high-street presence or function online. Location is key, and consignment stores' stock and customer base will vary, so shop around to find the best stores and shoppers for your products. What you gain from consignment stores – less hassle and access to more targeted customers – you lose in cash through commissions, which can be around 30 to 50 per cent. But you'll still be left with some cash in hand and a less full, more organized closet.

8

Return to the maker

You can even take your unwanted clothes back to where you bought them from! Not to be confused with take-back schemes (see p. 210), some designers and brands have such a strong commitment to a more sustainable fashion industry and taking ownership of their waste that they have created collection points where their customers can drop off clothes once they have finished with them. These forward-thinking companies (such as Filippa K and Patagonia) then do the reselling for you, either through secondhand rails in-store or in separate stores, reselling their own pre-worn designs. This type of selling helps to close the loop on the brand's products, but also ensures that your unwanted clothes return to the designers' captive customer base to be loved and worn all over again.

10

Rent out your wardrobe

Some of your barely worn clothes will be hard to say goodbye to forever. If you have valuable, quality items that you're not ready to let go of yet, how about renting? Renting is a great halfway house that allows you to capture your clothing's dormant value without a complete parting of the ways. Search online for the growing number of peer-to-peer clothing hire or rental websites, including Yeechoo and Rentez-Vous. Typically, these sites will allow you to list your garments for an administrative fee. The price shown to renters might include cleaning costs, and sometimes even covers insurance, meaning that your garment has a good chance of staying in good condition for when you want to wear it again, while also providing you with some income.

9

Sell in bulk

If you have lots of low-quality garments to sell, you could sell to clothing traders. Search online for 'cash for clothes'. But be forewarned that these traders aren't interested in making sure you get a generous profit: they buy per kilo and their prices are low. They then sort your cast-offs according to future use, from recycling and resale to possible export, so your unwanted clothes will be reused in some shape or form, rather than ending up in landfill.

ANNIE GEORGIA GREENBERG

Annie Georgia Greenberg is fashion editor-at-large for the Refinery29 website. She has worked for *Lucky*, *Vogue* and *Nylon* magazines, the *Chicago Tribune*, and marketing company Young & Rubicam, and can often be seen representing Refinery29 on air on VH1 and New York Live.

'Reselling clothes and buying vintage ones makes sense – financially, ecologically and aesthetically. Trends are cyclical, after all, so it's smart to sort through resale shops to find throwback styles you'll want to wear again, plus it's cheaper and better for the environment. And there's no arguing with the fact that an item feels more special when it's no longer in production. Selling clothes fits in with this ethos, too. The idea that something I've worn or travelled with could carry on afterwards is so cool and connecting. It takes on a new life and saves waste. Everyone wins!'

Annie's essentials for reselling

You can sell anything

You can have a go at selling almost anything, but vintage pieces, bags, jeans and branded items often sell more easily. Try not to be overly sentimental when choosing what clothes to resell. If you're on the fence, wear it again and see if it feels right. If not, sell it.

Go online!

As a fashion editor, my closet often gets an update. By reselling my clothes online, others can reap the benefits from what I no longer need. If you're looking to sell, try one of the many websites that connect you directly with customers around the world, or visit your local consignment store for those extra-valuable pieces.

Pricing is everything

Buyers love a good deal, but as the seller you want to ensure a decent price. Do your research and see what is selling, and at what price points. This will give you confidence in your own pricing. Alternatively, if you're selling through a consignment store that has a pricing guideline in place, you can rely on the experts to help you reach an amount that is fair.

Fashion editor Annie Georgia Greenberg's job means that she edits her own closet frequently, selling on clothes she no longer wears, whether online or through consignment stores.
(See her tips on p. 191)

'Finding people of similar size and a similar style ensures that your swapping will be more successful. Borrowing friends' clothes is another way to give your closet versatility without commitment.' – Lisa Corneliusson and Emma Elwin, Make It Last

Gift it

Our default gift-giving mode tends to be to buy something new, and clothes are up there as one of the most commonly gifted items. But gifting your unwanted clothes is a great way to be more inventive with your waste! Many of us have a 'boutique' of unworn clothes and accessories packing our closets that other people may truly appreciate.

Clean, complete, quality

Whether gifting to friends or to strangers, give quality clothes that match the receiver's style or needs. Repeat the mantra 'clean, complete and quality': you don't want your friends to feel you're simply off-loading your cast-offs or using them as a living rubbish bin. If your gift has a personal story, share it, because this will heighten your gift's value to the receiver. Your gift will have meaning for both of you and you'll get the pleasure of seeing your clothes enjoying a new life, while reducing your friend's need to buy new.

Open up your closet

With a little time and generosity, you can turn your unwanted clothes into meaningful gifts to help your wider community. Look out for posters and information at local churches, community centres, schools, clubs, sewing groups, rehabilitation centres or retirement homes. Depending on their circumstances, some may need clothes to wear or reuse. Think wool coats in winter for the homeless, or community centres that offer skill-building sewing classes and need materials to practise on. All you need is some imagination and the will to set your clothes free.

Set it free

Why not just give it away? If you have items to get rid of that you don't necessarily want to sell but do want to save from landfill, then post a free listing on a bulletin board at your local shop or community centre. Or go online: there are a few sites, such as The Freecycle Network, which allow you to reach a larger local audience. Alternatively, find a recycling centre where you can leave unwanted items for others who need them. This way, you help out your own community while reducing your closet's waste.

Donate it

Our closets are stuffed with value. But holding onto items you don't use anymore is bad for you and your wardrobe, and hoarding also holds back potential benefits for charities that help people in need. No matter what state your unwanted clothes are in, there are organizations out there that can benefit from them.

Understand the journey

There is a common misconception about what happens to your clothes after you donate them. Most of us assume they will end up with someone in need or sold to raise much-needed funds. While this is true in some cases, more often charities sell on donations, particularly poorer-quality items or those that aren't selling, to other companies, including commercial textile recyclers, to generate funds.

From there, the donated clothes may be sold again into other markets, especially in Africa and Southeast Asia where there are established secondhand markets. Ask how the charity processes incoming donations, and what happens to the clothes that don't sell. Read up on the issues to feel more informed about the destination of your donations, so that you feel comfortable with your choice of charity. Finally, take comfort in the knowledge that whatever charity you donate to, you are helping to redirect waste from landfill.

Choose a cause

Finding a charity that's close to your heart will make donating more meaningful. There are many to choose from, including charities that target education, helping the poor, child and animal welfare, human rights and environmental advocacy groups. Choosing your cause is an inspiring and insightful journey in itself, as you learn more about the issues that these groups are tackling.

To get going, find out what motivates and inspires you. Ask your friends for suggestions, look for local charitable organizations such as Friends of the Earth, the Red Cross or Cancer Research, or search online. Then contact your chosen charity or visit the shop to understand what types of donations are best and most needed. The more you know, the more your donations will match a particular charity's needs.

3

Get clothes resale-ready

Ensure your donations are fit for resale! Charities don't have the manpower or funding to launder or mend your donations, so if you really want to transform your unloved clothes into agents of change, check them over thoroughly before donating to ensure you generate the maximum value for your chosen charity.

4

Drop off with care ...

Charity shops rely on incoming donations to sell, so how effectively you donate is an important piece of the logistics puzzle that translates unwanted clothes into cash. Donation instructions will vary from shop to shop: some will accept donations in-store and others may want them dropped off nearer to sorting points. Be aware of the time you drop: don't leave donations out-of-hours, like a sartorial Santa Claus, because they may get rained on, or worse, stolen.

5

... and at your convenience

Some charities have collection points in public areas, like supermarket car parks or recycling facilities. These are usually large containers with secure, weatherproof chutes that prevent damage or theft. Yes, secondhand clothing is a profitable business! Charities will even partner with fashion brands, including Marks and Spencer and Zara, who place collection containers in their stores. But don't confuse these containers with other brand's own take-back schemes (see p. 210), which are usually for their own profit. When in doubt, read the small print.

6

Donate from your home

Occasionally, charities will organize door-to-door clothing collection services in their bid to collect more of your unwanted kit. Collection bags are dropped through your letterbox for you to fill with your unwanted clothes and leave outside for collection on a pre-determined date. Some charities may ask you to call to arrange collection, and others may outsource the logistics to another textile-collection service, which takes a cut of the profits.

If you want your charity to receive the full value of your clothing donations, find out if it is more profitable for them if you do the drop-off legwork yourself. As a final word of caution, you may wish to verify the charity is authentic by phoning or checking them out online. There have been cases of rogue clothing traders putting bogus 'charity' bags through letterboxes to get their hands on your valuable clothing waste.

'I wear mainly pre-loved, secondhand clothes. After I've loved and worn them even more, my unwanted clothes go back into the fashion loop. What comes around goes around, and that's why we're passionate about more sustainable closets at Redress.' – Christina Dean, Redress

'Sourcing clothes in more interesting and socially beneficial ways, through charity shops, swapping, lending or making connects us to people rather than material objects, and loosens advertising's grip on our style and identity.' – Leigh McAlea, TRAID

7 Bras for a cause

You may think some of your more intimate unwanted items, like old bras and pants, are worthless – but think again. Millions of women can't afford a bra and so are more than happy to wear yours. There are specific organizations, such as Bravissimo and Smalls for All, who seek out your secondhand items, which could get redirected to women in developing countries or sold to fund research. So send your intimates out into the world as champions for a cause.

8 Look out for clothing drives

Occasionally, charities will organize targeted clothing drives to collect donations. These could be regularly held drives or ad-hoc ones – in response to a disaster, for example – so keep your eyes open. If you feel passionate about a charitable cause, organize a clothing drive in your neighbourhood, local school or at work to encourage others to donate and to promote the conscious closet mindset further afield.

'When travelling to Zambia, I had a spare allowance
on my international flight. I'd heard of organizations
that collect donations from tourists in my situation,
and came across Project Luangwa, which provides
much-needed bras and sexual-health awareness to girls
who have been sexually abused. I was so inspired that
I collected 353 unwanted bras friends and colleagues
and flew them out myself.'

Sayeh Ghanbari

BONNIE CHEN

Model Bonnie Chen has graced catwalks and magazine covers around the world, and has worked with Christian Dior, Vivienne Tam, *Vogue* and *Elle* magazines. She is a former National Champion rhythmic gymnast and psychology graduate from the University of Pennsylvania. In 2012 she set up Star Bunny Love, and is an ambassador for the EcoChic Design Award sustainable fashion design competition.

'Working in the fashion industry, I've seen so much clothing waste created as we perpetually move onto the newest trends. Giving and selling unwanted clothes to charity is one way consumers can really help. I set up Star Bunny Love to fundraise for children with autism, a cause close to my heart. In China, public clothing-collection outlets aren't as common as in the West, and my fashion-loving friends really wanted their unwanted clothes to go to the right place. So I combined my passions, and this became a great opportunity to raise funds.'

Bonnie's essentials for clothing donation

Hold your own sale!

If your favourite charity doesn't have a reselling or recycling system, get others to donate clothes to help you convert unwanted clothes into money for your chosen cause.

Donations must be sale-ready

Clean your unwanted clothes, and make sure they're in a good state of repair. This ensures they go straight onto the hanger to be converted into cash and support your chosen charity.

Find a charity you believe in

Once you have found a charity that speaks to your heart and mind, contact it to make sure your unwanted clothes match its needs. Some charities need donations to give directly to people in crisis, others will resell donations themselves via charity sales or auctions to raise money, while still others will sell directly to recyclers.

Years of modelling her way through seasonal fashion trends led Bonnie Chen to search out more sustainable ways of disposing of perfectly good yet unwanted clothes through charity donation. (See her tips on p. 205).

The Makenew Curated Thrift Shop in Canada sells pre-owned garments and vintage finds alongside products by emerging designers of sustainable jewelry, accessories and homeware.

Hand waste to commercial recyclers

You may have unwanted items that seem destined for the bin, but think again. Textiles are almost 100 per cent recyclable, so no clothes should ever enter landfill. The problem is that too many people don't know about the multitude of businesses out there that welcome waste with open arms, which is partly why millions of tonnes of textiles are unnecessarily clogging up landfill when they could be transformed to have another useful life.

This is where commercial textile recyclers step in. They take in almost anything and make it easy for you to expel all of your unwanted clothes quickly and conveniently, so that you don't have to carefully sort your unwanted stash into specific waste streams if you don't have the time or inclination to do so.

1

Get informed

As their name suggests, commercial textile recyclers are money-making enterprises, so giving them your unwanted clothes doesn't generate charitable funds. Instead, most commercial recyclers will sell them on to other markets, which means that your clothing's real end use and destination are essentially unknown.

Your clothes could be resold as they are, or shredded for use as low-value stuffing materials, a process known as downcycling. A better option to prolong their use and make the most of already embedded resources is to upcycle them into products of higher quality, including transforming them back into clothes. Before handing over your old garments, ask where they will end up and what they will be used for. Don't be discouraged, because all commercial recycling is better than sending clothes to landfill.

2

Leave no trace of waste

Commercial recyclers are the vultures of recycling, they take anything – even old pyjamas and underpants. So don't worry if your unwanted items are broken, ripped, stained or seriously out of style, because commercial recyclers only see dollar signs. For them, reaching massive scale is key, and more really is more.

3

Take it back

You can also recycle while you shop! Take-back schemes are becoming more common, and a few of the bigger high-street brands, including Levi's, H&M and North Face, now have recycling containers in-store. Once you drop off your unwanted clothes, there are various routes they can then take. One is to be sold on to commercial textile recyclers for use in other markets around the world. Better-quality clothes may find themselves sold back into the secondhand market as they are.

If clothes are unable to be reused, they can be broken down into fibres and then respun into 'new' fabric. This recycling route is great for clothes that have reached the end of their lives, as it effectively reincarnates them, keeping all those initial resources already invested in the original garment in the fashion loop for longer. To tempt you further, some brands even give out vouchers to reward those who bring their clothes back to recycle, but don't let this be an excuse to fuel unnecessary consumption. Ask in-store or check your brand's website to find out more about take-back schemes.

Head to a recycling centre

Depending on where you live, you may have access to a recycling centre that accepts textiles. Typically, these are larger refuse centres run by local councils or independent companies, usually located outside towns and cities, whose sole purpose is to collect and manage different streams of our waste. You can usually drop off your unwanted clothes here for recycling, along with glass, paper and plastic, even your kitchen sink! As with all commercial recyclers, it's not always crystal-clear what happens to the clothes in their onward journey. But recycling is always a preferable option to sending your clothes to landfill. If you need help locating your recycling centre, check with your local council or district office.

Rethink it

At some stage, we end up with garments that are so stained, ripped and damaged that they are surely past their useful lives. Or we may have unwearable clothes that are so seeped in sentimental value we can't bear to part with them, and instead hide them away in a cupboard to be forgotten about.

But if you're feeling creative, and you want a gold medal for your conscious closet, there are ways to breathe new life into clothes that can't otherwise be swapped, resold or donated. With a little imagination and creativity, you can reuse many textiles around the home and continue the shift towards living a zero-waste life.

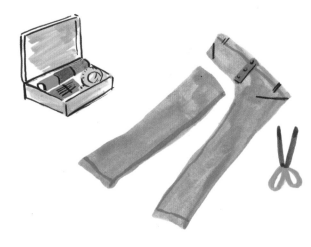

Repurpose garments ...

Just because a garment isn't suitable to wear doesn't mean it can't be repurposed. Damaged or sentimental items could be ripped up further and fashioned into quilts or woven into rugs. Or you could try framing sentimental and beautiful items – your favourite print scarf or your child's first babygrow – to bring well-loved pieces back into view as works of art. Finally, why not shred worn or damaged clothes to use as stuffing materials for cushions and toys? The only limit is your imagination.

'I love using discarded clothing as "paint" because it is creative, sustainable and a vehicle for transformation and healing. Making art with discarded clothes allows me to dismantle the world and piece it together again in a more pleasant way.'

Linda Friedman-Schmidt, artist

... or deconstruct them

With an open mind and a sharp eye, even a garment that might seem unwearable could have some functional or fashionable details worth salvaging. Deconstruct clothes that are beyond repair by salvaging buttons, zips or embellishments, which you can then add to your sewing kit. When you next come to repair (see pp. 156–61) or DIY (see pp. 90–5) other items in your wardrobe, you'll have more materials for inspiration and less need to hit the shops.

3

Turn clothes into rags

Why buy new cleaning cloths, which drive further textile production and cost money, when you can use your old clothes as rags? Natural fibres are good for cleaning because they are absorbent, so old cotton T-shirts, flannel PJs or towelling dressing gowns are perfect. Wash your car, polish your silver and scrub those windows! For the über-conscientious, you can even make your own mop by cutting cotton textiles into long strips and tying them on a wooden stick, moving ever closer to a conscious closet and home.

4

Use them in the garden

If you have non-biodegradable textiles that are high in polyester (such as blankets or old coats), place them around the base of plants to discourage weed growth or underneath pebbles and patio stones to reduce the need for chemical weed-killers. You could even line plant pots with a thin layer of unwanted clothes to keep the soil inside the pot while allowing water to drain out. All of the above gives redundant clothes the chance to last for another season.

Compost it

If your old clothes are made from all-natural materials, such as cotton, silk, linen or hemp, you can even add them to the compost heap. Eventually, the fibres will break down, along with your kitchen and garden waste, to become fertilizer. Shred your clothes to speed up the composting process. And as a final note, some clothes that claim to be made from 100 per cent natural fibres can include polyester threads and trims, which aren't biodegradable. Although the phrase 'needle in a haystack' springs to mind, you could pick over the compost heap and collect the polyester threads once the fabric has broken down.

MALIN PERSSON

Interior stylist Malin Persson spent 15 years as a model, working for fashion labels including Chanel, Dior, Givenchy and Dolce & Gabbana. She has also presented *Scandinavia's Top Model*, and opened a successful book bar, Salotto 42, while living in Rome. After returning to Sweden, Malin's work as an interior stylist has been featured in magazines, on television and on her popular blog for *Elle Decoration*.

'We need to move away from the idea that products are disposable and towards a more sustainable way of living. We are too quick to get rid of the old and bring in the new without considering their emotional and environmental value. Around 80 per cent of the items in my home are secondhand, and I rarely buy anything new. Instead, when I want a change I move around what I already have and try to find new ways of using things. I also store items in my basement and pack some away, which allows me to rediscover them afresh a few months later.'

Malin's essentials for reuse

Turn your clothes into art

Enjoy the true beauty of clothes. There's no need to shove them to the back of the wardrobe just because you don't wear them anymore. Hang beautiful garments in a window, on a wall or on the outside of your wardrobe, so that they can be admired while giving your home a personal touch at the same time. I hung my wedding gown on my bedroom wall for years to remind me of one of the happiest moments of my life.

Don't let anything go to waste

Even if your clothes are no longer wearable, you can reuse them in your home. Worn-out clothes such as jeans are very durable and can be cut up to make cushions or reupholster a chair.

Rethink function

When an item of clothing or an accessory is no longer useful in its original form, try using it in a completely new way. High-heeled shoes that are worn out or simply too uncomfortable to walk in can be used as bookends, and a favourite silk nightgown can be turned into a luxurious curtain.

Malin Persson brings her discerning style to everything from her kitchen to her kimonos. She is passionate about finding sustainable alternatives – such as chairs made from unwanted denim – and has a keen eye for all things vintage. (See her tips on p. 217).

Believing in guilt-free consumption and committed to a circular economy, MUD Jeans encourages customers to send back purchases at the end of their life. These are then recycled into new products, such as this sweater, made from 84 per cent-recycled denim.

1. How can the fashion industry become more sustainable? (2015, March 29). Retrieved from www.businessoffashion.com/community/voices/discussions/can-fashion-industry-become-sustainable.

2. Streamlined life cycle assessment of two Marks & Spencer apparel products (2002, February). Retrieved from https://researchingsustainability.files.wordpress.com/2012/01/streamlined-lca-of-2-marks-spencer-pls-apparel-products.pdf.

3. Hower, M. (2013, April 29). Nike, NASA, US State Department and USAID seek innovations to revolutionize sustainable materials. Retrieved from www.sustainablebrands.com/news_and_views/articles/nike-nasa-us-state-department-usaid-seek-innovations-revolutionize-sustainab.

4. Reducing the environmental impact of clothes cleaning (2009, December). Retrieved from randd.defra.gov.uk/Document.aspx?Document=EV0419_8628_FRP.pdf.

5. *The True Cost* (film), 2015; Consumer wealth and spending: The $12 trillion opportunity (2012). Retrieved from www.atkearney.com/documents/10192/278946/consumer+wealth+and+spending.pdf.

6. Jan Whitaker, *Service and Style: How the American Department Store Fashioned the Middle Class* (New York: St Martin's Press, 2006); Trends: An annual statistical analysis of the US apparel and footwear industries (2009, August). Retrieved from www.wewear.org/assets/1/7/Trends2008.pdf.

7. Davis, R. (2006, October 9). How to say no to impulse buys. Retrieved from www.redbookmag.com/life/money-career/advice/a255/impulse-buys-yl/.

8. Westwood, R. (2013, May 1). What does that $14 shirt really cost? Retrieved from www.macleans.ca/economy/business/what-does-that-14-shirt-really-cost.

9. International trade statistics 2014. Retrieved from www.wto.org/english/res_e/statis_e/its2014_e/its14_toc_e.htm.

10. Cotton (2016). Retrieved from pan-uk.org/organic-cotton/wearorganic-homepage.

11. Water stewardship for industries: The need for a paradigm shift in India (2013, March 1). Retrieved from http://re.indiaenvironmentportal.org.in/reports-documents/water-stewardship-industries-need-paradigm-shift-india.

12. Figures based on 16 pairs of jeans, from Deloitte, *Fashioning Sustainability 2013.*

13. Globalization changes the face of textile, clothing and footwear industries (1996, October 28). Retrieved from www.ilo.org/global/about-the-ilo/newsroom/news/WCMS_008075/lang--en/index.htm.

14. Smith, R.A. (2013, April 17). A closet filled with regrets. Retrieved from www.wsj.com/articles/SB10001424127887324240804578415002232186418.

15. Bye, E., and E. McKinney (2015, April 21). Sizing up the wardrobe: Why we keep clothes that do not fit. Retrieved from www.tandfonline.com/doi/abs/10.2752/175174107X250262.

16. Valuing our clothes (2012). Retrieved from www.wrap.org.uk/sites/files/wrap/VoC%20FINAL%20online%202012%2007%2011.pdf.

17. Ibid.

18. Streamlined life cycle assessment of two Marks & Spencer apparel products (2002, February).

19. Valuing our clothes (2012).

20. Clothes washers (energystar.gov/products/appliances/clothes_washers).

21. Mercola, J. (2012, May 13) The worst ingredients in laundry detergent. Retrieved from www.care2.com/greenliving/the-worst-ingredients-in-laundry-detergent.html.

22. United States Environmental Protection Agency, 2012.

23. Valuing our clothes (2012).

24. Lucy Siegle, *To Die For: Is Fashion Wearing Out the World?* (London: Fourth Estate, 2011).

25. Municipal solid waste in the United States: 2011 facts and figures (2011). Retrieved from https://nepis.epa.gov/Exe/ZyNET.exe/P100GMT6.TXT.

26. Less is more: resource efficiency through waste collection, recycling and reuse (2013). Retrieved from www.foeeurope.org/sites/default/files/publications/foee_report_-_less_is_more_0.pdf.

27. China Association of Resource Comprehensive Utilization, 2013.

28. Recycling post-consumer textiles (2001). Retrieved from http://cordis.europa.eu/result/rcn/80681_en.html.

29. Donate, recycle, don't throw away! (n.d.) Retrieved from www.smartasn.org/educators-kids/SMARTInfographtextileRecycling.pdf.

30. Recycling of low grade clothing waste (2006, September). Retrieved from www.oakdenehollins.co.uk/pdf/defr01_058_low_grade_clothing-public_v2.pdf.

31. University of Copenhagen, 2008.

32. Valuing our clothes (2012).

33. Textiles (n.d.). Retrieved from www.bir.org/industry/textiles.

34. Measuring biodegradability (2008). Retrieved from http://sciencelearn.org.nz/Contexts/Enviro-imprints/Looking-Closer/Measuring-biodegradability.

35. Valuing our clothes (2012).

Biodegradable
A material's ability to be decomposed ecologically.

Carbon footprint
The volume of gas emissions measured as a result of production and consumption activities.

Certification
A formal procedure to confirm certain characteristics of an object, person or organization.

CO_2 emissions
Released into the atmosphere along with other gases, including methane, by burning fossil fuels such as gas, coal and oil.

Corporate social responsibility (CSR)
A policy developed by a company that sets out its environmental and ethical aims, goals and standards.

Fairtrade
Supports social developments by paying fair prices for goods and services, while reinvesting profit back into the local community.

Fast-fashion
Low-cost, low-quality clothing that has been rapidly produced to replicate catwalk trends.

Green-washing
A term given to misleading, exaggerated or untrue claims about a product's environmental benefits.

Organic
Clothing and textiles made using environmentally friendly processes, from field to manufacture.

Reconstruction
The process of making new clothes from previously worn garments or preformed products.

Recyclable
Materials that can be reused and turned into a new, usable material or product.

Recycled
A waste material or product that has been reused and turned into a new usable material or product.

Responsible consumerism
Choosing to purchase products and services that take into account their social and environmental impacts.

Secondhand
Clothing, textiles and fashion accessories and textiles that have been used and discarded by consumers.

Supply chain
The steps and resources involved in moving a product from raw material to consumer.

Swap/swish
A form of direct recycling through swapping of unwanted garments.

Tencel
A biodegradable manmade fibre made out of wood pulp cellulose.

Upcycling
The recycling of a material into a product of higher quality.

Zero-waste
A design technique that eliminates textile waste at the design stage.

We have done the hard work for you, and pulled together some of our favourite and most useful sites, books, films, brands and organizations. Head to the websites listed to find out more.

REDRESS
redress.com.hk/dresswithsense
facebook.com/RedressAsia
instagram.com/GetRedressed

GET INSPIRED
Blogs and online publications
Conscious Living TV
consciouslivingtv.com
Conscious
consciousmagazine.co
Ecouterre
ecouterre.com
Fashion Me Green
fashionmegreen.com
Guardian Sustainable Business
theguardian.com/us/
sustainable-business
Make It Last
makeitlast.se
Sublime
sublimemagazine.com
Trash is for Tossers
trashisfortossers.com
Zero-Waste Home
zerowastehome.com

Books and film
Sandy Black, *The Sustainable Fashion Handbook* (London and New York, 2012).
Greta Eagan, *Wear No Evil: How to Change the World with Your Wardrobe* (Philadelphia, 2014).
Frontline Fashion (documentary), 2016
Safia Minney, *Slow Fashion* (Northampton, UK, 2016).

Lucy Siegle, *To Die For: Is Fashion Wearing Out the World?* (London, 2011).
The True Cost (dir. Andrew Morgan), 2015.
Geneva Vanderzeil, *DIY Fashionista: 40 Stylish Projects to Reinvent and Update Your Wardrobe* (London, 2012).

Organizations
Ethical Fashion Forum
ethicalfashionforum.com
Fashion Revolution
fashionrevolution.org
Greenpeace: Detox our Future
greenpeace.org
Nice Fashion
nordicfashionassociation.
com/nice

People
Orsola de Castro
twitter.com/orsoladecastro
Christina Dean
instagram.com/drchristinadean
Livia Firth
instagram.com/livia_firth
Camilla Marinho
instagram.com/damn_project
Safia Minney
twitter.com/SafiaMinney
Summer Rayne Oakes
instagram.com/srmanitou
Amber Valletta
instagram.com/ambervalletta
Matteo Ward
instagram.com/matteo.ward
Marci Zaroff
instagram.com/marcizaroff

BUY
Brands
Christopher Raeburn
christopherraeburn.co.uk
EcoChic Design Award alumni

(Angus Tsui, Katie Jones, Wan & Wong Fashion, Farrah Floyd, ï Miss Sophïe, Benu Berlin, Alex Leau, Classics Anew, Awa Awe, Tiffany Pattinson, Leif Erikkson, Clémentine Sandner, Norst, WindausWister)
ecochicdesignaward.com/
alumni
Edun
edun.com
Eileen Fisher
eileenfisher.com
Everlane
everlane.com
FEED
feedprojects.com
Freitag
freitag.ch
Goodone
goodone.co.uk
Honest by
honestby.com
Johanna Ho
johannaho.com
Knotti
knotti.co
Kuyichi
kuyichi.com
Matt & Nat
mattandnat.com
MUD Jeans
mudjeans.eu
Nudie Jeans
nudiejeans.com
O My Bag
omybag.nl
Pants to Poverty
pantstopoverty.com
Patagonia
patagonia.com
People Tree
peopletree.co.uk
Reformation
thereformation.com

(Re)vision Society
  revisionsociety.com
Stella McCartney
  stellamccartney.com
Study 34
  study34.co.uk
Tengri
  tengri.co.uk
Timberland
  timberland.co.uk
TOMS
  toms.com
Veja
  veja-store.com
Vetta
  shopvetta.com
Wool and the Gang
  woolandthegang.com

Online retailers
A Boy Named Sue
  aboynamedsue.co
ASOS (Eco Edit)
  asos.com
Master & Muse
  masterandmuse.com
Not Impossible
  buyimpossible.com
Rêve en Vert
  revenvert.com
Shopethica
  shopethica.com
Yooxygen
  yoox.com/us/project/yooxygen
Zady
  zady.com

Renting
Bag Borrow or Steal
  bagborroworsteal.com
Lena: The Fashion Library
  lena-library.com
Le Tote
  letote.com
L'Habibliothèque
  lhabibliotheque.com

Rentez Vous
  rentez-vous.com
Rent the Runway
  renttherunway.com
Yeechoo
  yeechoo.com

Secondhand
Beyond Retro
  beyondretro.com
Fertha
  fertha.com
The Hula
  thehula.com
Vinted
  vinted.co.uk

Environmental standards
bluesign
  bluesign.com
Ecocert
  ecocert.com
Fairtrade
  fairtrade.net
Global Organic Textile Standard
  global-standard.org
Global Recycle Standard
  textileexchange.org
Soil Association
  soilassociation.org

WEAR
Wardrobe organizing
Closet
  closetapp.com
Cloth
  clothapp.com
Marie Kondo
  konmari.com/app
My Dressing
  mydressing.co
Stylebook
  stylebookapp.com
Stylitics
  stylitics.com

DIY inspiration
A Pair & A Spare
  apairandasparediy.com
I Spy DIY
  ispydiy.com
P.S. – I Made This
  psimadethis.com
Trash to Couture
  trashtocouture.com

Redesign inspiration
Beth Huntington, *Refashion
  Handbook: Refit, Redesign,
  Remake for Every Body*
  (Concord, California, 2014).
Henrietta Thompson, *Remake
  It Clothes: The Essential
  Guide to Resourceful Fashion*
  (London and New York,
  2012).
New Dress A Day
  newdressaday.com
Sew Over It
  sewoverit.co.uk

CARE
Repairing inspiration
*Singer Simple Mending and
  Repair: Essential Machine-side
  Tips and Techniques* (London,
  2007).
Joan Gordon, *Stitch 'n' Fix:
  Essential Mending Know-
  how for Bachelors and Babes*
  (Lewes, East Sussex, 2009).
Patagonia Repair & Care Guides
  patagonia.com/us/worn-wear-
  repairs
The Good Wardrobe
  thegoodwardrobe.com

Washing
Blanc
  blancclean.com
Clever Care
  clevercare.info

DIY Natural
diynatural.com

Ecover
ecoverdirect.com

Method
methodhome.com

Mr Black
mr-blacks.com

Seventh Generation
seventhgeneration.com

The Laundress
thelaundress.com

The Simply Co.
thesimplyco.com

Tangent GC
tangentgc.com

Washologi
washologi.se

DISPOSE

Swapping sites

Freecycle
freecycle.org

Global Fashion Exchange
globalfashionexchange.org

The Clothes Club
theclothesclub.info

The Clothing Exchange
clothingexchange.com.au

Vinted
vinted.com

Resale platforms

BuyMyWardrobe
buymywardrobe.com

eBay
ebay.com

Guiltless
guiltless.com

Poshmark
poshmark.com

The Vestiaire Collective
vestiairecollective.com

thredUP
thredup.com

Tradesy
tradesy.com

Companies collecting clothes
& Other Stories
stories.com

Bravissimo
bravissimo.com

Filippa K
Filippa-k.com

H&M
hm.com

Levi's
levistrauss.com

Marks & Spencer
marksandspencer.com

Nike
nike.com

North Face
thenorthface.com

Patagonia
patagonia.com

Reformation
thereformation.com

Uniqlo
uniqlo.com

Zara (select stores)
zara.com

Return to maker

Filippa K
filippaksecondhand.se

MUD Jeans
mudjeans.eu

Charities collecting clothes

Cancer Research
cancerresearchuk.org

Friends of the Earth
foe.co.uk

Goodwill
goodwill.org

Oxfam
oxfam.org

Red Cross
redcross.org.uk

Salvation Army
salvationarmy.org

TRAID
traid.org.uk

Charities collecting specific items

Dress for Success
dressforsuccess.org

Free The Girls
freethegirls.org

Soles4Souls
soles4souls.org

Wish Upon a Wedding
wishuponawedding.org

Wrap Up London
wrapuplondon.org.uk

PHOTO CREDITS

24, 54 Butcher Casey; 25
Issa Ng; 44 Courtesy of
Reformation; 45 Larry
Hirshowitz; 55 Alex Salinas;
64, 107 Rachel Manns; 65t
ASOS; 65b Shovan Gandhi;
80 Sam Wong for A Boy
Named Sue; 81 Susanna Lau;
98–9 Geneva Vanderzeil;
106 Naïmsiu Photography;
124 Jeff Johnson/Patagonia;
125 The Simply Co.; 142
Kenneth Nguyen; 143 Lindsey
Bell Photography; 150 Charl
Marais; 151 Luke Casey; 164
Kotur; 165 Darren Mulryan;
192 Refinery29; 193 Emma
Elwin; 200 Redress/Sherman
Wong; 201 Hannah Lane;
206 Raul Docasar, design by
Karen Jesson for The Redress
Forum: Designer Challenge
with Miele; 207 Lindsay
Duncan/Makenew; 218 Malin
Persson and Mia Anderberg,
styling by Malin Persson; 219
MUD Jeans